Learning C# 7 By Developing Games with Unity 2017

Third Edition

Learn C# Programming by building fun and interactive games with Unity

Micael DaGraça

Greg Lukosek

BIRMINGHAM - MUMBAI

Learning C# 7 By Developing Games with Unity 2017

Third Edition

First published: September 2013

Second edition: March 2016

Third edition: December 2017

Production reference: 1211217

Published by Packt Publishing Ltd.
Livery Place
35 Livery Street
Birmingham
B3 2PB, UK.
ISBN 978-1-78847-892-2

www.packtpub.com

Credits

Author
Micael DaGraça
Greg Lukosek

Reviewers
Predrag Koncar

Commissioning Editor
Amarabha Banerjee

Acquisition Editor
Reshma Raman

Content Development Editor
Flavian Vaz

Technical Editor
Ralph Rosario

Copy Editor
Safis Editing

Project Coordinator
Devanshi Doshi

Proofreader
Safis Editing

Indexer
Pratik Shirodkar

Graphics
Jason Monteiro

Production Coordinator
Melwyn Dsa

About the Authors

Micael DaGraça is a game designer and an AR developer living in Porto, Portugal. He has worked for multiple game studios, contributing to the creation of different indie games and interactive apps. Micael grew up playing video games, and that passion never went away. So later on, in his life, he decided to learn how to create games. Without any previous knowledge in coding or 3D animation, he slowly started creating simple games, learning more with those experiences each time. When the games began working fine and the gameplay became enjoyable, he started making plans to publish a game in collaboration with an old friend. Micael was responsible for the technical aspect of the game, ensuring that the game worked as planned, while his friend created all the artwork for the game. Finally, the game was published, and it received some positive feedback from other indie game developers. Since the game generated some revenue, the decision of becoming a game designer turned into reality. Today, Micael works for other studios, helping others to develop their game ideas, He has also integrated into a company that focuses on the creation of interactive apps for health care and pharmaceutic companies. Even not having time to keep working on personal projects, he has a few frozen game projects that are still under development with the help of his friend.

> *"First and most importantly, I would like to thank my parents; they have always worked so hard and I know that they sacrificed a lot so I could pursue my dreams. From the bottom of my heart I thank you mom and dad. To my sister who has supported me in so many ways, I thank you for helping me start my career as a game designer; without you, my journey would be much harder. A warm and fluffy thank you to my girlfriend Marta, who helps me by keeping me motivated and focused on my work; it's been more than a pleasure sharing my life with you."*

Greg Lukosek was born and raised in the Upper Silesia region of Poland. When he was about 8 years old, his amazing parents bought him and his brother a Commodore C64. That was when his love of programming started. He would spend hours writing simple basic code, and when he couldn't write it on the computer directly, he used a notepad.

Greg completed his mechanical engineering diploma at ZSTiO Meritum–Siemianowice Slaskie, Poland. He has learned all his programming skills through determination and hard work at home.

Greg met the love of his life, Kasia, in 2003, which changed his life forever. They both moved to London in search of adventure and decided to stay there.

He started work as a 3D artist and drifted away from programming for some years. Deep inside, he still felt the urge to come back to game programming. During his career as a 3D artist, he discovered Unity and adopted it for an interactive visualizations project. At that very moment, he started programming again.

His love for programming overcomes his love for 3D graphics. Greg ditched his 3D artist career and came back to writing code professionally. He is now doing what he really wanted to do since he was 8 years old–developing games.

These days, Greg lives in a little town called Sandy in the UK with Kasia and their son, Adam.

About the Reviewer

Predrag Koncar is a game developer/artist and multimedia researcher, active in both visual arts and computer science. His primary areas of interest are games and combining technology and art. He likes to spend his free time painting and actively participates in art shows. Predrag has worked as a technical and creative director for many online projects, published over 40 online games, participated in the production of several mobile games, and also reviewed five books by Packt Publishing. He has a strong background in Unity, C#, Augmented Reality, Maya, and AI and is a member of Mensa and ACM SIGGRAPH.

www.PacktPub.com

For support files and downloads related to your book, please visit `www.PacktPub.com`.

Did you know that Packt offers eBook versions of every book published, with PDF and ePub files available? You can upgrade to the eBook version at `www.PacktPub.com` and as a print book customer, you are entitled to a discount on the eBook copy. Get in touch with us at `service@packtpub.com` for more details.

At `www.PacktPub.com`, you can also read a collection of free technical articles, sign up for a range of free newsletters and receive exclusive discounts and offers on Packt books and eBooks.

`https://www.packtpub.com/mapt`

Get the most in-demand software skills with Mapt. Mapt gives you full access to all Packt books and video courses, as well as industry-leading tools to help you plan your personal development and advance your career.

Why subscribe?

- Fully searchable across every book published by Packt
- Copy and paste, print, and bookmark content
- On demand and accessible via a web browser

Customer Feedback

Thanks for purchasing this Packt book. At Packt, quality is at the heart of our editorial process. To help us improve, please leave us an honest review on this book's Amazon page at https://www.amazon.com/dp/1788478924.

If you'd like to join our team of regular reviewers, you can e-mail us at customerreviews@packtpub.com. We award our regular reviewers with free eBooks and videos in exchange for their valuable feedback. Help us be relentless in improving our products!

Table of Contents

Preface   1

**Chapter 1: Discovering Your Hidden Scripting Skills and Getting Your
Environment Ready**   7

  Prerequisite knowledge to use this book   8
  Dealing with scriptphobia   8
  Downloading Unity   9
    Obtaining a free license   10
  Teaching behavior to GameObjects   10
    Using Unity's documentation   11
    The Unity community – asking others for help   14
  Working with C# script files   14
  Creating a C# script file   15
  Introducing the MonoDevelop code editor   15
    Opening LearningScript in MonoDevelop   17
      The namespace – highlighted in blue   18
    Watching for possible gotchas while creating script files in Unity 18
    Fixing synchronization if it isn't working properly   20
    Adding our script to GameObject   20
    Lots of files can create a mess   22
    Why does my Project tab look different?   22
  Instance? What is this?   25
  Summary   25

Chapter 2: Introducing the Building Blocks for Unity Scripts   27

  Understanding what a variable is and what it does   28
    Naming a variable   28
    A variable name is just a substitute for a value   32
    Creating a variable and seeing how it works   34
      Declaration   35
      Assignment   36
    Click Play!   36
    Changing variables   37
    Watching for a possible gotcha when using public variables   37
  What is a method?   38
    Using the term "method" instead of "function"   38

Method names are substitutes, too	40
Introducing the class	41
Inheritance	43
The Start(), Update(), and Awake() methods, and the execution order	44
Components that communicate using dot syntax	46
What's with the dots?	46
Making decisions in code	47
Using the NOT operator to change the condition	48
Checking many conditions in an if statement	49
Using else if to make complex decisions	49
Making decisions based on user input	51
Pencil and paper are powerful tools	52
Summary	52
Chapter 3: Getting into the Details of Variables	53
Writing C# statements properly	54
Understanding component properties in Unity's Inspector	55
Variables become component properties	55
Unity changes script and variable names slightly	55
Changing a property's value in the Inspector panel	56
Displaying public variables in the Inspector panel	57
Private variables	57
Naming your variables properly	58
Beginning variable names with lowercase	59
Using multiword variable names	59
Declaring a variable and its type	60
The most common built-in variable types	61
Assigning values while declaring a variable	61
Where you declare a variable is important	63
Variable scope - determining where a variable can be used	64
Summary	65
Chapter 4: Getting into the Details of Methods	67
Using methods in a script	68
Naming methods properly	69
Beginning method names with an uppercase letter	69
Using multiword names for a method	69
Parentheses are part of the method's name	70
Defining a method the right way	70
The minimum requirements for defining a method	70

Understanding parentheses - why are they there?	72
Specifying a method's parameters	73
How many parameters can a method have?	74
Returning a value from a method	74
Returning the value	75
Example	76
Summary	78

Chapter 5: Lists, Arrays, and Dictionaries — 79

What is an array?	79
Declaring an array	80
Storing items in the List	81
Common operations with Lists	83
List <T> versus arrays	83
Retrieving the data from the Array or List<T>	84
Checking the size	85
ArrayList	85
Dictionaries	87
Accessing values	88
How do I know what's inside my Hashtable?	89
Summary	89

Chapter 6: Loops — 91

Introduction to loops	91
The foreach loop	92
The for loop	94
An example	95
The while loop	99
while versus for loops	100
Loops in statements	100
Modulo	102
Searching for data inside an array	103
Breaking the loop	104
Summary	104

Chapter 7: Object, a Container with Variables and Methods — 105

Working with objects is a class act	105
A few facts	108
Example	110
Instantiating an object	111
Bored yet?	113

Using methods with objects   114
Custom constructors   116
Overloading   118
Summary   120

Chapter 8: Let's Make a Game! – from Idea to Development   121
    Your first game – avoiding the trap of the never–ending concept   121
    What do I need to learn before I start creating my own game?   122
       The concept   123
    Game mechanics and core components   123
    Breaking the concept into smaller parts   124
    Testing the mechanics   126
       Level design   126
       An animated 2D character   127
       Physics   128
       Mouse and touch controls   128
       Collectables and obstacles   128
       Scoring   129
       UI – the user interface   130
    Target platform and resolution   132
    Target screen resolution   133
    Summary   133

Chapter 9: Starting Your First Game   135
    Setting up a new Unity project for our game   136
       Backup   136
       Keeping your project clean   137
    Preparing the player prefab   139
       Rigidbody2D   141
       CircleCollider2D   142
    PlayerController   143
    User input   144
       Jump   145
    Animator   151
       Running   153
    Code   154
       PlayerController.cs   154
    Summary   155

Chapter 10: Writing GameManager   157

Gameplay loops   157
Singleton class   160
Starting the game   162
Setting up input keys   163
Using triggers   164
Restarting the game   167
Setting up the player starting position   167
Code in this chapter   169
Summary   172

Chapter 11: The Game Level   173
Designed levels versus generated levels   173
Creating a designed level   175
Creating a generated level   179
   Planning the LevelGenerator class   180
   Writing the script LevelGenerator   182
Creating a copy of the level piece   184
Instantiating   185
Vector3   185
Testing LevelGenerator   187
Extending the level   188
The code used in this chapter   190
Summary   192

Chapter 12: The User Interface   193
Introducing the Unity UI   194
Views   194
   Constructing the view UI – how to keep things clean   194
   Target screen resolution   195
   Recognizing events   196
Buttons   198
   Basic button   199
      The image   199
      The Button component   199
      Interaction   200
      The Button action   200
Hiding and showing the Canvas   202
Reference exceptions   203
GameView   206
   Game over   207
The code in this chapter   208

Summary   210

Chapter 13: Collectables   211

Collectables   211
The coin prefab   212
   The Collectable class   216
High score and persisting data   219
Health Points and Health bar   221
Magic Points and Magic bar   223
The code in this chapter   224
Summary   231

Chapter 14: Enemies   233

What makes an enemy?   233
Movement   234
   Movement by animation   234
   Trigger movement   238
   Making it an enemy   244
The code in this chapter   245
Summary   249

Chapter 15: Audio, 3D Games, and Export   251

How to add sound effects and music   251
   Where to find sound effects and music   251
   Adding music   252
   Adding sound effects   256
      Through animation   257
      Through script   259
How to create a 3D game   260
   3D models   261
   3D animations   261
   Animator   263
How to export and make it playable   265
Code   267
   PlayerController.cs   268
Summary   270

Index   271

Preface

Hello and welcome to the amazing journey of game development. This book is destined for those who have always wanted to create a game, the ones who have thousands of good ideas for games and people who inspire to be professional game developers. This book is destined for you. Here, you will learn the fundamentals of how to create a game from start to finish using Unity and C#. Step by step, you will be learning how to code and how to use the game engine to turn your ideas into real projects. At the end of the book, you'll have created a 2D platform game, and you will know how to create different games using the same principles that you have learned.

What this book covers

Chapter 1, *Discovering Your Hidden Scripting Skills and Getting Your Environment Ready*, puts you at ease with writing scripts for Unity.

Chapter 2, *Introducing the Building Blocks for Unity Scripts*, helps you develop the skill of writing your first executable code.

Chapter 3, *Getting into the Details of Variables*, teaches you about creating and using C# variables, followed editing them in Unity Inspector.

Chapter 4, *Getting into the Details of Methods*, helps you learn more in detail about methods and how to use them to understand the importance of code blocks and the variables used in them.

Chapter 5, *Lists, Arrays, and Dictionaries*, introduces slightly more complex ideas of handling, lists, arrays, and dictionaries, which allow you to store many values at once.

Chapter 6, *Loops*, focuses on learn how to "ask" Unity to loop through a section of code and do something useful.

Chapter 7, *Objects, a Container with Variables and Methods*, dives into the subjects of organizing your code and object-oriented programming.

Chapter 8, *Let's Make a Game! – from Idea to Development*, explains how to turn an idea into a ready-to-code project and how to break down complex mechanics into pieces.

Chapter 9, *Starting Your First Game*, outlines transforming an idea into a real Unity project.

Chapter 10, *Writing GameManager*, gets you acquainted with the basics of the singleton approach and also helps you work through the gameplay loop.

Chapter 11, *The Game Level*, teaches how to create reusable pieces of a level and also how to populate them to create the illusion of an endlessly running game.

Chapter 12, *The User Interface*, showcases how to construct and implement the user interface in our game.

Chapter 13, *Collectables*, outlines collectables and storing some data between Unity sessions.

Chapter 14, *Enemies*, assists in how to create enemies and obstacles, how to animate them and how to turn simple Game Objects into deadly objects.

Chapter 15, *Audio, 3D Games, and Export*, assists in implementing audio effects and music, introduces you to the fundamentals of how to create a 3D game, and finally, how we can export the game to multiple platforms.

What you need for this book

You will definitely need a computer–PC, Mac, or any machine that supports Unity editor installation. The complete Unity system requirements can be found at https://unity3d.com/unity.

Who this book is for

The book is targeted at beginner-level Unity developers with no prior programming experience. If you are a Unity developer and wish to create games by learning how to write C# scripts or code, then this book is for you.

Conventions

In this book, you will find a number of text styles that distinguish between different kinds of information. Here are some examples of these styles and an explanation of their meaning.

Code words in text, database table names, folder names, filenames, file extensions, pathnames, dummy URLs, user input, and Twitter handles are shown as follows: "This is the part where you have to write down instructions so that your GameObjects can be smarter."

A block of code is set as follows:

```
void AddTwoNumbers ()
{
  // Code goes here
}
```

New terms and **important words** are shown in bold. Words that you see on the screen, for example, in menus or dialog boxes, appear in the text like this: "Go ahead and click **Play**."

Warnings or important notes appear in a box like this.

Tips and tricks appear like this.

Reader feedback

Feedback from our readers is always welcome. Let us know what you think about this book-what you liked or disliked. Reader feedback is important for us as it helps us develop titles that you will really get the most out of.

To send us general feedback, simply e-mail feedback@packtpub.com, and mention the book's title in the subject of your message.

If there is a topic that you have expertise in and you are interested in either writing or contributing to a book, see our author guide at www.packtpub.com/authors.

Customer support

Now that you are the proud owner of a Packt book, we have a number of things to help you to get the most from your purchase.

Downloading the example code

You can download the example code files for this book from your account at http://www.packtpub.com. If you purchased this book elsewhere, you can visit http://www.packtpub.com/support and register to have the files e-mailed directly to you.

You can download the code files by following these steps:

1. Log in or register to our website using your e-mail address and password.
2. Hover the mouse pointer on the **SUPPORT** tab at the top.
3. Click on **Code Downloads & Errata**.
4. Enter the name of the book in the **Search** box.
5. Select the book for which you're looking to download the code files.
6. Choose from the drop-down menu where you purchased this book from.
7. Click on **Code Download**.

You can also download the code files by clicking on the **Code Files** button on the book's webpage at the Packt Publishing website. This page can be accessed by entering the book's name in the **Search** box. Please note that you need to be logged in to your Packt account.

Once the file is downloaded, please make sure that you unzip or extract the folder using the latest version of:

- WinRAR / 7-Zip for Windows
- Zipeg / iZip / UnRarX for Mac
- 7-Zip / PeaZip for Linux

The code bundle for the book is also hosted on GitHub at https://github.com/PacktPublishing/Learning-C-7-By-Developing-Games-with-Unity-2017-Third-Edition. We also have other code bundles from our rich catalog of books and videos available at https://github.com/PacktPublishing/. Check them out!

Errata

Although we have taken every care to ensure the accuracy of our content, mistakes do happen. If you find a mistake in one of our books-maybe a mistake in the text or the code-we would be grateful if you could report this to us. By doing so, you can save other readers from frustration and help us improve subsequent versions of this book. If you find any errata, please report them by visiting http://www.packtpub.com/submit-errata, selecting your book, clicking on the **Errata Submission Form** link, and entering the details of your errata. Once your errata are verified, your submission will be accepted and the errata will be uploaded to our website or added to any list of existing errata under the Errata section of that title.

To view the previously submitted errata, go to https://www.packtpub.com/books/content/support and enter the name of the book in the search field. The required information will appear under the **Errata** section.

Piracy

Piracy of copyrighted material on the Internet is an ongoing problem across all media. At Packt, we take the protection of our copyright and licenses very seriously. If you come across any illegal copies of our works in any form on the Internet, please provide us with the location address or website name immediately so that we can pursue a remedy.

Please contact us at copyright@packtpub.com with a link to the suspected pirated material.

We appreciate your help in protecting our authors and our ability to bring you valuable content.

Questions

If you have a problem with any aspect of this book, you can contact us at questions@packtpub.com, and we will do our best to address the problem.

1
Discovering Your Hidden Scripting Skills and Getting Your Environment Ready

Computer programming is viewed by the average person as requiring long periods of training to learn skills that are totally foreign and darn near impossible to understand. The word *geek* is often used to describe a person who can write computer code. The perception is that learning to write code takes great technical skills that are just so hard to learn. This perception is totally unwarranted. You already have the skills needed but don't realize it. Together, we will crush this false perception that you may have of yourself by refocusing, one step at a time, on the knowledge that you already possess to write code and develop an awesome game from scratch.

In this chapter, we will cover the following topics:

- Dealing with preconceived fears and concepts about scripts
- Preparing the Unity environment for efficient coding
- Introducing Unity's documentation for scripting
- Explaining how Unity and the MonoDevelop editor work together
- Creating our first C# script

Let's begin our journey by eliminating any anxiety about writing scripts for Unity and become familiar with our scripting environment.

Prerequisite knowledge to use this book

Great news if you are a beginner in scripting! This book is for those with absolutely no knowledge of programming. It is devoted to teaching the basics of C# with Unity.

However, some knowledge of Unity's operation is required. We will only be covering the parts of the Unity interface that are related to writing C# code. I am assuming that you know your way around Unity's interface. I will help you, however, to prepare the Unity layout for efficient scripting.

Dealing with scriptphobia

You've got Unity up and running, studied the interface, and added some `GameObjects` to the scene. Now you're ready to have those `GameObjects` move around, listen, speak, pick up other objects, shoot the bad guys, or do anything else that you can dream of. So you click **Play**, and nothing happens. Well, darn it all anyway!

You've just learned a big lesson: all those fantastic, highly detailed `GameObjects` are dumber than a hammer. They don't know anything, and they surely don't know how to do anything.

So, you proceed to read the Unity **Forums**, study some scripting tutorials, and maybe even copy and paste some scripts to get some action going when you click **Play**. That's great, but then you realize that you don't understand anything in the scripts you've copied. Sure, you probably recognize the words, but you fail to understand what those words do or mean in a script.

You look at the code, your palms get sweaty, and you think to yourself, "I'll never be able to write scripts!" Perhaps you have *scriptphobia*: a fear of not being able to write instructions (I made that up). Is that what you have?

The fear that you cannot write down instructions in a coherent manner? You may believe you have this affliction, but you don't. You only think you do.

The basics of writing code are quite simple. In fact, you do things every day that are just like the steps executed in a script. For example, do you know how to interact with other people? How to operate a computer? Do you fret so much about making a bologna sandwich that you have to go to an online forum and ask how to do it?

Of course you don't. In fact, you know these things as everyday routines or maybe habits. Think about this for a moment: do you have to consciously think about the routines that you do every day? Probably not. After you do them over and over, they become automatic.

The point is that you do things every day following sequences of steps. Who created these steps that you follow? More than likely, you did, which means that you've been scripting your whole life.

You just never had to write down the steps for your daily routines on a piece of paper before you did them. You could write the steps down if you really wanted to, but it takes too much time and there's no need for it; however, you do in fact know how to. Well, guess what? To write scripts, you only have to make one small change, start writing down the steps, not for yourself but for the world that you're creating in Unity.

So as you can see, you are already familiar with the concept of dealing with scripts. Most beginners of Unity easily learn their way around the Unity interface, how to add assets, and working in the Scene and Hierarchy windows. Their primary fear and roadblock is their false belief that scripting is too hard to learn.

Relax! You now have this book. I am going to get really basic in the early chapters. Call them baby steps if you want, but you will see that scripting for Unity is similar to doing things that you are already doing every day. I'm sure you will have many *Aha* moments as you learn and overcome your unjustified fears and beliefs.

Downloading Unity

You have probably already installed and activated Unity. Where you should look for the latest Unity version and license might be obvious. However, I've noticed lots of questions online about where you can get Unity for free, and so I decided to cover this subject. If you feel that this step is unnecessary for you, skip this part.

The best place to download your Unity copy from is, of course, Unity's official website: `https://store.unity.com/download?ref=personal`.

In this book, we will be covering Unity Version 2017.1.1 and higher. We need to download the latest version of Unity and install it with all components ticked. It's a good idea to install Unity with the example project. The Unity Example project (the *Angry Bots* game) is there for us to play with, experiment, and learn.

Unity has a store where we can also download more example projects and start playing around with them. To access the store, you can do it online or directly from the Unity engine, so don't worry if you forgot to check the Unity Example project in the installation menu because you can download it at any time.

Obtaining a free license

The easiest way to obtain a Unity license is by simply launching Unity for the first time. The following steps will guide you through it:

1. Fill in your details so that Unity Technologies can send you your Unity free license code.
2. Unity will present the **License management** window. Chose the **Unity Personal** (free version).
3. You should receive a verification email with a **Confirm email** button. Once you have clicked it, you should be able to log in to Unity.

You are now all set with the latest version of Unity and a free license!

Teaching behavior to GameObjects

You have Unity because you want to make a game or something interactive, such as an AR or VR experience. You've filled your game with dumb GameObjects. What you have to do now is be their teacher. You have to teach them everything that they need to know to live in this world of make–believe. This is the part where you have to write down instructions so that your GameObjects can be smarter.

Here's a quote from the *Unity Manual*:

> *"The behavior of GameObjects is controlled by the Components that are attached to them... Unity allows you to create your own Components using scripts."*

Notice the word *behavior*. It reminds me of a parent teaching a child proper behavior. This is exactly what we are going to do when we write scripts for our GameObjects: we'll teach them the behaviors we want them to have. The best part is that Unity has provided a long list of all the behaviors that we can give to our GameObjects. This list of behaviors is documented in the **Scripting Reference**.

This means that we can pick and choose anything that we want a `GameObject` to do from this list of behaviors. Unity has done all the hard work of programming all of these behaviors for you. All we need to do is use some code to tie into these behaviors. Did you catch that? Unity has already created the behaviors; all that we have to do is supply a bit of C# code to apply these behaviors to our `GameObjects`. Now, how difficult can it really be since Unity has already done most of the programming?

Using Unity's documentation

When we begin writing scripts, we will be looking at Unity's documentation quite often, so it's beneficial to know how to access the information we need. For an overview of a topic, we'll use the *Reference Manual*, and for specific coding details and examples, we'll use the **Scripting Reference**.

There are a number of ways to access the Unity documentation:

- Through the Unity website at
  `http://docs.unity3d.com/ScriptReference/index.html`.
- Through the **Help** menu on the top bar. In this way, you can access a local copy of Unity reference as we can see in the following image. This is worth remembering if there are internet connectivity issues:

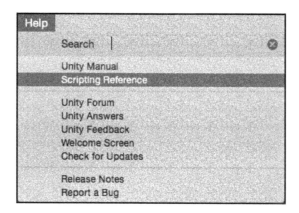

- Let's open **Scripting Reference** now and search for a GameObject:

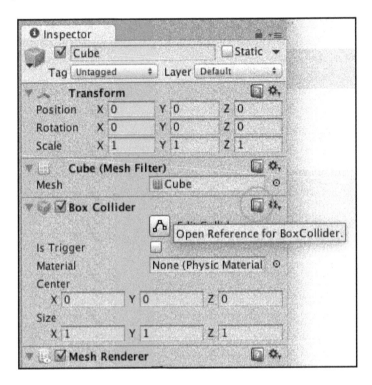

- Through the **Help** menu next to the component name. This will work only for Unity's built-in, standard components.

This is the place where we can find scripting documentation, answers to our questions, and a lot of example code. You might feel a bit lost right now, but don't worry, this is quite normal. The Unity documentation is really easy to use. For the fastest access to relevant information, use **Search scripting...** in the top–right corner, as shown here:

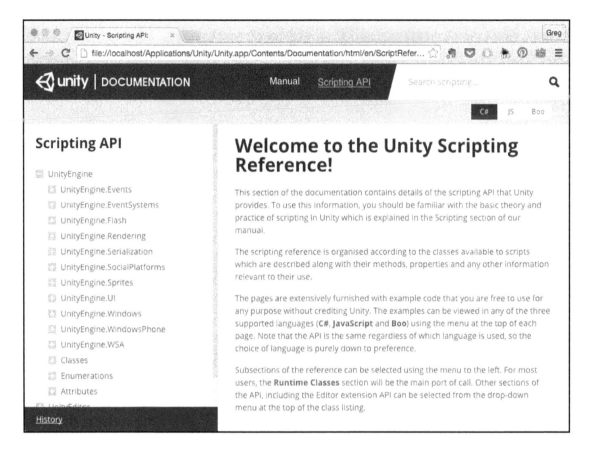

 The whole reason **Scripting Reference** exists is so that we can look for information as we need it. This will actually make us remember the code that we write over and over, just like our other daily routines and habits. It is a very good idea to take a brief look through the most common Unity objects, such as GameObject, Transform, MonoBehaviour, and Renderer.

C# documentation – where to find it and do I need it at all?

Another resource that we will be using is Microsoft's C# scripting documentation. We can access it at `https://msdn.microsoft.com/en-us/library/67ef8sbd.aspx`.

Let's not worry about it too much at the moment. We agreed to take baby steps, so bookmark this link in your web browser for now.

The Unity community – asking others for help

You are planning to become a game developer, or are using Unity for other interactive projects. During production, at some point, you will definitely need help from other developers. Unity has a very dedicated community of developers who are always keen to help each other.

When we encounter some hurdles, why not ask others? In most cases, there is someone like you out there with similar issues that have been resolved. A good place to talk about issues in your project is in the Unity **Forums**. Go ahead and create a forum account now! Don't be shy; say "hello" to others! Unity **Forums** are also the perfect place to read announcements about upcoming updates.

Use Unity **Forums** to read about others' work, share your work, and connect with other developers at `http://forum.unity3d.com/`.

Use Unity **Answers** to ask specific questions about issues that you have encountered. Remember to be very specific, try to describe the problem in detail, and don't ask general questions. For example, don't ask, "Why is my `GameObject` not moving?" Instead, ask specifically, "`GameObject` not moving when adding a rigid body force" and then describe the details. Posting your code under the question is also a very good idea.

Working with C# script files

Until you learn some basic concepts of programming, it's too early to study how scripts work, but you still need to know how to create one.

There are several ways of creating a script file using Unity:

1. In the menu, navigate to **Assets** | **Create** | **C# Script**
2. In the Project tab, navigate to **Create** | **C# Script**
3. Right-click on the **Project** tab, and from the pop–up menu, navigate to **Create** | **C# Script**

All of these ways create a `.cs` file in the Unity `Assets` folder. From now on, whenever I tell you to create a C# script, use whichever method you prefer.

Creating a C# script file

We are now ready to create a new C# file in our learning project:

1. Create a new Unity project and name it `Learning Project`
2. Right-click on the **Project** tab and create a folder named `Scripts`
3. Right-click on the `Scripts` folder, as shown in the following screenshot, and create a C# script:

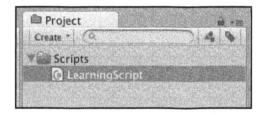

4. Immediately rename `NewBehaviourScript` to `LearningScript`

We have created the `Scripts` folder, which we will be using to organize our C# files. This folder will contain all of our Unity script files. We have also used Unity to create a C# script file named `LearningScript.cs`.

Introducing the MonoDevelop code editor

Unity uses an external editor to edit its C# scripts. Even though it can create a basic starter C# script for us, we still have to edit the script using the MonoDevelop code editor that's included with Unity.

Syncing C# files between MonoDevelop and Unity

Since Unity and MonoDevelop are separate applications, Unity will keep MonoDevelop synchronized with itself. This means that if you add, delete, or change a script file in one application, the other application will reflect the changes automatically.

It is possible to also choose another code editor if we want to. For example, web developers can keep using their favorite editor if they choose to do so. If you feel more comfortable using another code editor, you can do it by following these steps:

1. Go to the **Preferences** menu that can be found under the **Unity** tab on Mac, or the **Edit** tab on Windows
2. Select **External Tools**:

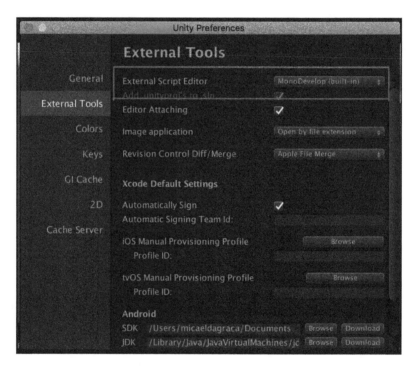

3. Under the **External Script Editor** option, you can browse for the application that you want to use as the code editor:

Opening LearningScript in MonoDevelop

Unity will synchronize with MonoDevelop the first time you tell it to open a file for editing. The simplest way to do this is by double-clicking on **LearningScript** in the Scripts folder (provided in the example project). If your project is empty, don't worry, you can create a new C# script that will contain the exact same information. To do it, you just need to right-click inside the **Assets** tab and select **Create | C#Script**. It might take a few seconds for MonoDevelop to open and sync.

Our window should look like this:

MonoDevelop launched with **LearningScript** open and ready to edit.

What we see now is a default C# script structure that Unity creates. It contains information on what namespaces are used in the script, the class definition, and two methods that Unity adds by default, as shown here:

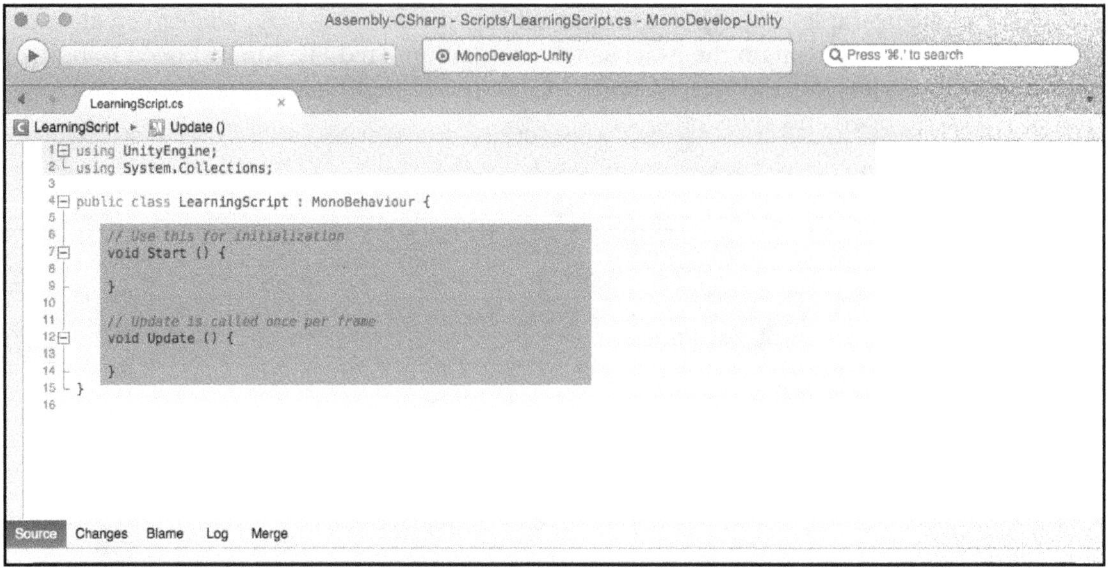

The namespace – highlighted in blue

The namespace is simply an organizational construct. It helps organize parts of code. Don't worry too much about it now. We won't need to create them anytime soon. All we will need to know for now is how many namespaces we are using in our script.

In our script, we can see these two lines:

```
using UnityEngine;
using System.Collections;
```

The preceding two lines simply mean that our script will be using the `UnityEngine` and `System.Collections` namespaces, and we will have access to all parts of these libraries. These two namespaces are added to any new C# script by default, and we will use them in most of our cases.

Watching for possible gotchas while creating script files in Unity

Notice line **4** in the following screenshot:

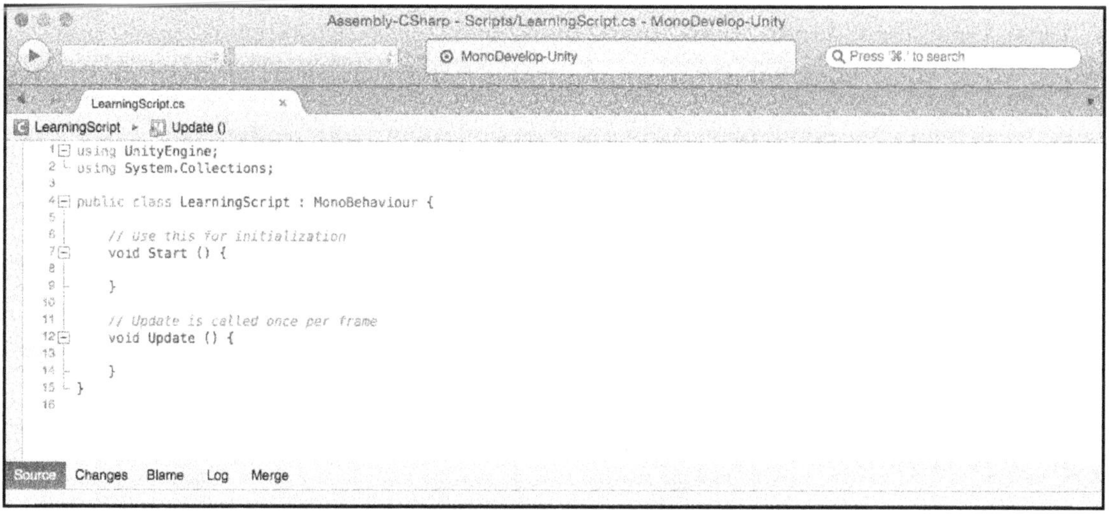

```
public class LearningScript : MonoBehaviour
```

The class name `LearningScript` is the same as the filename `LearningScript.cs`. This is a requirement. You probably don't know what a class is yet, but that's okay. Just remember that the filename and the class name must be the same.

When you create a C# script file in Unity, the filename in the **Project** tab is in **Edit** mode, ready to be changed. Please rename it right then and there. If you rename the script later, the filename and the class name won't match. The filename would change, but line **4** will be this:

```
public class NewBehaviourScript : MonoBehaviour
```

This can easily be fixed in MonoDevelop by changing `NewBehaviourScript` in line **4** to the same name as the filename, but it's much simpler to do the renaming in Unity immediately.

Fixing synchronization if it isn't working properly

What happens when Murphy's Law strikes and syncing just doesn't seem to be working correctly? Should the two apps somehow get out of sync as you switch back and forth between them for whatever reason, do this. Right–click on Unity's **Project** window and select **Sync MonoDevelop Project**. MonoDevelop will resync with Unity.

Adding our script to GameObject

We have created the `LearningScript` class. Its code is saved in the file in the **Project/Scripts** folder. To include an instance of this class in our project, we will add it as a component to an empty `GameObject`.

Let's create a new `GameObject`. In the menu, navigate to **GameObject** | **Create Empty Child**, as shown here:

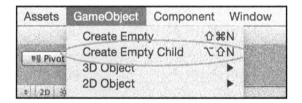

There are a number of ways of adding our `LearningScript` component to the `GameObject`. Let's talk about the simplest one:

1. Select your newly created `GameObject`:

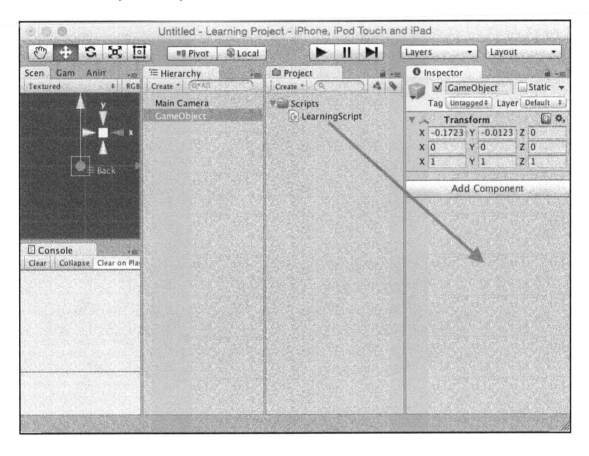

2. Drag and drop the `Script` file from the **Project** tab to the empty space underneath the **Transform** component:

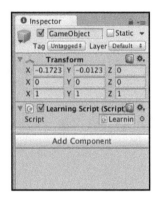

We can now see that our `LearningScript` file has been added as a component to the `GameObject`. This means that an instance of `LearningScript` is active and ready to execute code.

Lots of files can create a mess

As our Unity project progresses, we will have lots of different types of files in the **Project** view. It's highly recommended that you keep a clean and simple folder structure in your project.

Let's keep our scripts in the `Scripts` folder, textures in `Textures`, and so on, so that it looks something like this:

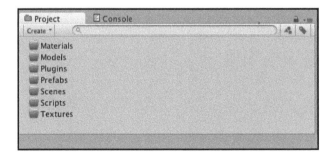

From now on, let's not keep any loose files in the `Assets` folder.

Why does my Project tab look different?

Unity allows us to customize the user interface. Everyone has their own favorite. I prefer a one–column layout **Project** tab instead of Unity's default two–column layout. To change this, open the context menu in the top-right corner of the **Project** tab, as shown in this screenshot:

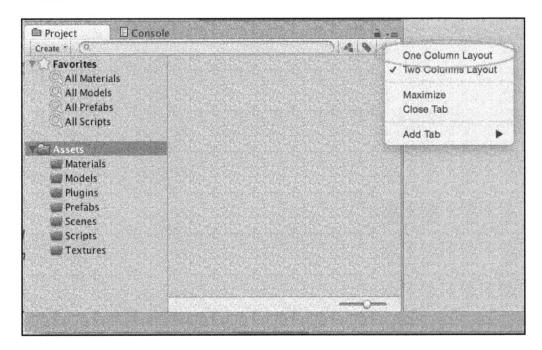

When working in a team, you will notice that every team member has their own layout preference. A level designer may like to use a big **Scene** tab. An animator will probably use the **Animation** and **Animator** tabs. For a programmer like you, all tabs are fairly important. However, the **Console** tab is the one that you will use a lot while testing your code. I mostly prefer a layout divided into four columns from left to right, **Scene**, and **Console**, then **Hierarchy**, then **Project**, and finally **Inspector**.

It looks like what is shown in the following screenshot:

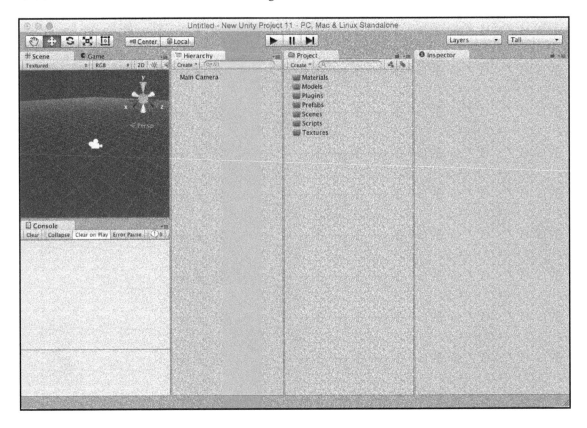

 If you have trouble with moving tabs around, refer to the *Customizing Your Workspace* chapter in the *Unity Manual*.

Feel free to change the interface however you want. But try to keep the **Console** tab visible all the time. We will use it a lot throughout the book. You can also save your custom layouts in the **Layout** menu.

 The **Console** tab shows messages, warnings, errors, or debug output from your game. You can define your own messages to be sent to the console.

Instance? What is this?

In object-oriented programming, an instance is simply a copy of the object. In this case, there is one copy of our `LearningScript` file. We are using two terms here: `GameObject` and Object. Do not mix these up, they are, in fact, two different things. `GameObject` is an object in your Unity scene. It contains components such as **Transform** or our newly created `LearningScript`.

Object in programming means an instance of the script. Don't worry about the terminology too much at this stage. I am sure that the difference between these two will become much clearer soon.

Summary

This chapter tried to put you at ease with writing scripts for Unity. You do have the ability to write down instructions, which is all a script is, just a sequence of instructions. We saw how simple it is to create a new script file. You probably create files on your computer all the time. We also saw how to easily bring forth Unity's documentation. We created a channel to communicate with other developers. Finally, we took a look at the MonoDevelop editor. None of this was complicated. In fact, you probably use apps all the time that do similar things. The bottom line: there's nothing to fear here.

In `Chapter 2`, *Introducing the Building Blocks for Unity Scripts*, we will start off introducing the building blocks for Unity scripts by taking an introductory look at the building blocks of programming. For this, we'll be using variables, methods, dot syntax, and classes. Don't let these terms scare you. The concepts behind each one of these are similar to things that you do often, perhaps every day.

2

Introducing the Building Blocks for Unity Scripts

The C# programming language can appear to be very complicated at first, but in reality, there are two basic parts that form its foundation. These parts are variables and methods. Therefore, understanding these critical parts is necessary to learn any of the other features of C#. As critical as they are, they are very simple concepts to understand. Using these variable and method foundation pieces, we'll introduce the C# building blocks that are used to create Unity scripts.

For those who get sweaty palms just thinking of the word script, wipe your hands and relax! In this chapter, I'm going to use terms that are already familiar to you to introduce the building blocks of programming. The following are the concepts introduced in this chapter:

- Using variables and methods in scripts
- The class, which is a container for variables and methods
- Turning a script into a component
- Components that communicate using the dot syntax
- Making decisions in code

Understanding what a variable is and what it does

What is a variable? Technically, it's a tiny section of your computer's memory that will hold any information that you put there. While a game is running, it keeps track of where the information is stored, the value kept there, and the type of that value. However, for this chapter, all you need to know is how a variable works. It's very simple.

What's usually in a mailbox, besides air? Well usually there's nothing, but occasionally there is something in it. Sometimes, there are letters, bills, a spider, and so on. The point is that what is in a mailbox can vary. Therefore, let's call each mailbox a variable.

In the game development world, some simple examples of variables might be:

- `playerName`
- `playerScore`
- `highestScore`

Naming a variable

Using the example of the mailbox, if I asked you to see what is in the mailbox, the first thing you'd ask is, "Which one?" If I say in the Smith mailbox, the brown mailbox, or the round mailbox, you'll know exactly which mailbox to open to retrieve what is inside it. Similarly, in scripts you have to give your variables a unique name. Then I can ask you what's in the variable named `myNumber`, or whatever cool name you might use.

Let's see how this is represented in our code. The first thing we need to do is create a new script in Unity, all the fun and magic starts here from these first steps:

1. In the Unity project panel, under the **Assets** tab, we are going to right–click the empty space:

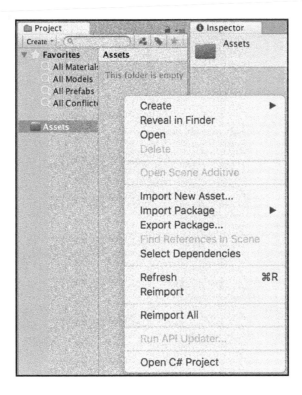

2. Then we go to the **Create** menu and select the **C# Script** option

3. A new file was created and it is ready to be renamed; this is very important and we need to always give a name to this file. For now, we can call it `variableScript` (the name we gave to this file doesn't interfere with the content on it, so we can we choose any name we want):

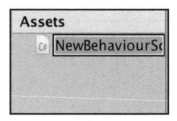

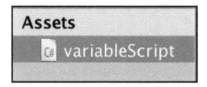

4. Then we double-click the script file that we have just created.
5. The MonoDevelop program will open with the script ready to edit:

```
     variableScript.cs                    ×

 variableScript  ▶  No selection

 1 using System.Collections;
 2 using System.Collections.Generic;
 3 using UnityEngine;
 4
 5 public class variableScript : MonoBehaviour {
 6
 7     // Use this for initialization
 8     void Start () {
 9
10     }
11
12     // Update is called once per frame
13     void Update () {
14
15     }
16 }
17
```

6. Make sure that the name that appears after `public` class is exactly the same name that you assigned inside Unity (in this example, we gave the name `variableScript`). In case we don't rename the script file right away when it gets created, Unity will automatically assign the `NewBehaviourScript` name:

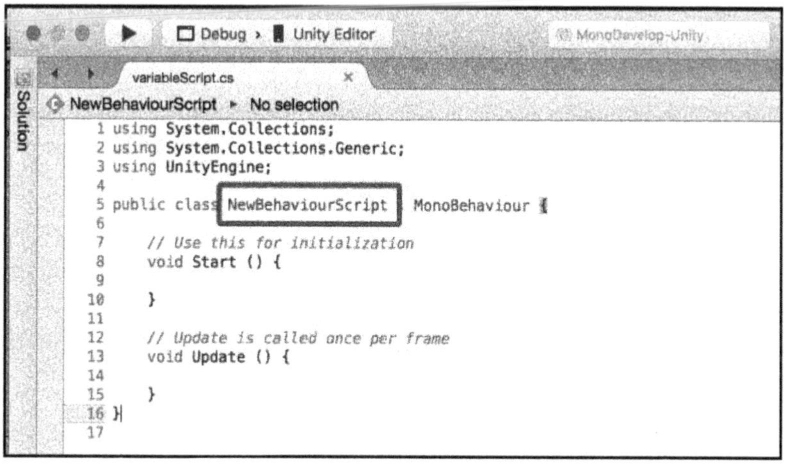

7. Now we are ready to create our first variable, we are going to name it `myNumber`. Make sure that your script looks identical to the following screenshot (for now, don't be concerned about the details of how to write this):

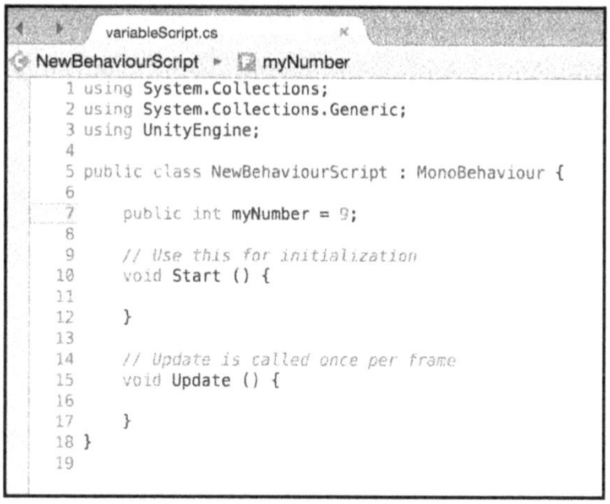

8. Save the file.

The golden rule: When you name variables, try to come up with a name that most accurately describes what value your variable contains. Avoid generic names such as name, speed, and score. Instead, name them playerName, carSpeed, and opponentScore, respectively.

A variable name is just a substitute for a value

As you write a script and create a variable, you are simply creating a placeholder or a substitute for the actual information that you want to use. Look at the following simple math equation: *2 + 9 = 11*.

Simple enough! Now try the following equation: *11 + myNumber = ???*. There is no answer to this. You can't add a number and a word. Going back to the mailbox analogy, write the number 9 on a piece of paper. Put it in the mailbox named myNumber. Now you can solve the equation. What's the value in myNumber? The value is 9. So now the equation looks normal: *11 + 9 = 20*.

The myNumber variable is nothing more than a named placeholder that can store some data (information). So, wherever you would like the number 9 to appear in your script, just write myNumber and the number 9 will be substituted.

We can test this on the script that we had previously created, so let's do it:

1. We start by selecting the script that we have created and then we double–click it to open inside MonoDevelop:

2. Now we create a new variable called total and we don't need to assign any number to it because we want this variable to show us the result of our:

```
public class variableScript| : MonoBehaviour {

    public int myNumber = 9;
    public int total;
```

3. After the `void Start ()` function, we are going to write the math equation `total = 2 + myNumber`:

```
// Use this for initialization
void Start () {
    total = 2 + myNumber;|
}
```

4. Save the file, go back to the Unity program, and drag and drop the script file on top of the **Main Camera** object:

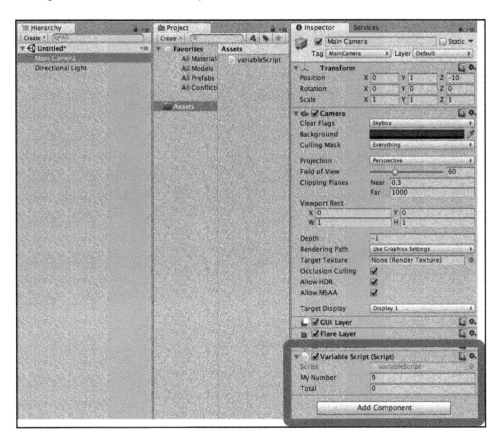

5. Click **Play** and take a look at the **Total** variable:

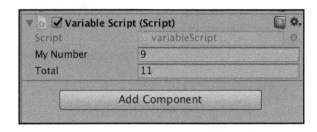

Although this example might seem silly at first, variables can store all kinds of data that is much more complex than a simple number. This is just a simple example that shows you how a variable works. We will definitely look at more complex variable types at later stages. Remember, slow, steady progress, baby steps!

Creating a variable and seeing how it works

Now using a different method, we are going to develop a script that shows us the result on the Unity console. Once again, don't be concerned about the details of how to write this; we are going to explain everything in more detail in future chapters. Just make sure that your script is the same as the script shown in the next screenshot:

1. In the Unity **Project** panel, double-click `variableScript`. The MonoDevelop window should open automatically on `variableScript.cs`.
2. In MonoDevelop, erase what we have done before and write the lines **7**, **12**, and **14**, as shown in the following screenshot:

```
1 using System.Collections;
2 using System.Collections.Generic;
3 using UnityEngine;
4
5 public class variableScript : MonoBehaviour {
6
7     public int myNumber = 9;
8
9     // Use this for initialization
10    void Start () {
11
12        Debug.Log (2 + 9);
13
14        Debug.Log (11 + myNumber);
15    }
16
17    // Update is called once per frame
18    void Update () {
19
20    }
21 }
22
```

3. Save the file.

 The best way to save your script is by using a shortcut. If you are using a Mac, use *command + S*, and on Windows use *Ctrl + S*. We will be saving a new version of the script every time some changes are made to it, so it is a good idea to use a shortcut instead of saving through the **File** menu.

We have added a few lines to our script. Before we check whether it works or what it actually does, let's go through line **7**:

```
public int myNumber = 9;
```

In simple words, this line declares a new number type variable named `myNumber` and assigns a value of 9 to it. We don't want to worry about theory too much now and want to write more code, right? Agreed, but we do need to remember a few things first.

Declaration

To create a new variable, we first need to declare it by saying what type of variable it is, and as we explored before, a variable type represents the content. This means that the content for the `myNumber` variable is a number. The keyword for whole number variables in C# is `int` and for different types of content, we assign a different keyword. We also have to give our variable a name; `myNumber` is fine for now. You can use any name you want, as long as it does not contain spaces or special characters.

Assignment

We have created our variable, and now we are giving it a value. To assign a value, we use the equals sign followed by the value. In this case, it is 9. To close the line, use a semicolon; this is always necessary. The program reads our script one line of code at a time, and by using the semicolon we are telling the program that the line of code ends there.

Click Play!

Quite an exciting moment! Go back from MonoDevelop to Unity and click the **Play** button. Unity should print out two lines on the **Console** tab, looking like this:

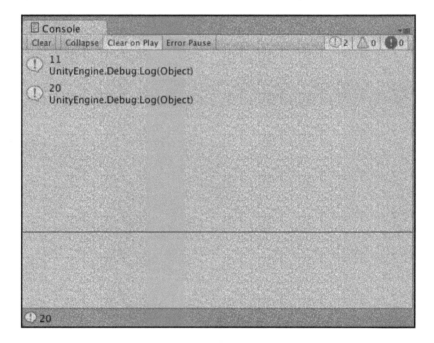

Unity executed the code in the `variableScript` component on the `GameObject` just after you clicked **Play**. We can see two lines printed on the **Console** window. We wrote a piece of code asking Unity to print these two values the **Console** window. Let's look again at lines **11** and **13**. Everything inside the brackets in the `Debug.Log` function will be printed to the Unity **Console**. It can be a number, text, or even an equation:

```
11                  Debug.Log(2 + 9);
12
13                  Debug.Log(11 + myNumber);
```

So, line **11** is asking, "Hey Unity, print the result of 2 + 9 on the console!" Line **14** is using the `myNumber` variable's value directly and adding it to the number 11.

Thus, the point of this exercise is to demonstrate that you can store and use whatever values you want using variables, and use their names directly to perform operations.

Changing variables

Since `myNumber` is a variable, the value that it stores can vary. If we change what is stored in it, the answer to the equation will also change. Follow these steps:

1. Stop Unity by pressing the **Stop** button and change 9 to 19 in the Unity **Inspector** tab
2. Notice that when you restart the game, the answer will be 30

I bet you have noticed the `public` keyword at the very beginning of the line that declares the `myNumber` variable. Let me explain what it means. It's called an **access modifier**. We use these to specify the accessibility of a variable. The `public` keyword means that the variable can be seen by code outside our script. Look again at the Unity **Inspector** tab. You can see the value of `myNumber` there because it is public. The private keyword, however, means that the variable can be accessed only by code in the same class.

 Private variables are not visible in the Unity **Inspector** tab. If you wish to control or view them, make them public.

Watching for a possible gotcha when using public variables

Unity gives us great flexibility with editing or reading public variables in the **Inspector** tab. You will be using public variables most of the time. Now, I want to make you aware of something that might give you a headache sometimes.

All public variable values are overridden by the Unity **Inspector** tab.

Let's look back at line **6**; we had assigned our variable a value of 9. This value will be copied to the Unity **Inspector**. From now on, the value from **Inspector** is taken into account and not the value in the script, even if you change it. Therefore, be careful as this is very easy to forget.

In the **Inspector** panel, try changing the value of myNumber to some other value, even a negative value. Notice the change in the answer in the **Console** tab.

What is a method?

When we write a script, we are making lines of code that the computer is going to execute, one line at a time. As we write our code, there will be things that we want our game to execute more than once. For example, we can write a piece of code that adds two numbers. Suppose our game needs to add those two numbers a hundred different times during gameplay. So you'd say, "Wow! I have to write the same code a hundred times to add two numbers together? There has to be a better way."

Let a method take away your typing pain. You just have to write the code to add two numbers once and then give this chunk of code a name, such as AddTwoNumbers(). Now, every time your game needs to add two numbers, don't write the code over and over, just call the AddTwoNumbers() method.

Using the term "method" instead of "function"

You are going to see the words "function" and "method" used everywhere as you learn how to code.

 The words "function" and "method" truly mean the same thing in Unity. They also do the same thing.

Since you are studying C#, and C# is an **Object–Oriented Programming** (**OOP**) language, I will use the word *method* throughout this book, just to be consistent with C# guidelines. It makes sense to learn the correct terminology for C#. The –Oriented Programming (OOP)">authors of **Scripting Reference** probably should have used the word "method" instead of "function" in all of their documentation. Anyway! Whenever you hear either of these words, remember that they both mean the same thing.

 From now on, I'm going to use the word method or methods in this book. When I refer to the functions shown in **Scripting Reference**, I'm going to use the word "method" instead, just to be consistent.

We're going to edit the `variableScript` again. In the following screenshot, there are a few lines of code that look strange. We are not going to get into the details of what they mean in this chapter. We will discuss that in Chapter 4, *Getting into the Details of Methods*. Right now, I am just showing you a method's basic structure and how it works:

1. In **MonoDevelop**, select `variableScript` for editing
2. Edit the file so that it looks exactly like what is shown in the following screenshot:

```
1   using UnityEngine;
2   using System.Collections;
3
4   public class LearningScript : MonoBehaviour {
5
6       public int number1 = 2;
7       public int number2 = 9;
8
9       // Use this for initialization
10      void Start () {
11
12      }
13
14      // Update is called once per frame
15      void Update () {
16          if (Input.GetKeyUp(KeyCode.Return)) AddTwoNumbers();
17      }
18
19
20      void AddTwoNumbers() {
21
22          Debug.Log( number1 + number2);
23      }
24
25  }
26
```

3. Save the file

In the previous screenshot, lines **6** and **7** will look familiar to you. They are variables, just as you learned in the previous section. There are two of them this time. These variables store the numbers that are going to be added.

Line **16** may look very strange to you. Don't concern yourself right now with how it works. Just know that it's a line of code that lets the script know when the *Enter* key is pressed. On the keyboard method, `AddTwoNumbers` will be called into action.

The simplest way to call a function in your code is by using its name followed by brackets and a semicolon, for example, `AddTwoNumbers();`.

Method names are substitutes, too

You learned that a variable is a substitute for the value that it actually contains. Well, a method is no different. Take a look at line **20** in the previous screenshot:

```
void AddTwoNumbers ()
```

`AddTwoNumbers()` is the name of the method. Like a variable, `AddTwoNumbers()` is nothing more than a named placeholder in the memory, but this time, it stores some lines of code instead. So, wherever we want to use the code in this method in our script, we just write `AddTwoNumbers()` and the code will be substituted.

Line **20** has an opening curly bracket and line **23** has a closing curly bracket. Everything between the two curly brackets is the code that is executed when this method is called in our script. Look at line **16** from the previous screenshot, precisely at this part:

```
AddTwoNumbers();
```

The method named `AddTwoNumbers()` is called. This means that the code between the curly brackets is executed. Of course, this `AddTwoNumbers()` method has only one line of code to execute, but a method can have many lines of code.

Line **22** is the action part of this method–the part between the curly brackets. This line of code adds the two variables and displays the answer on the Unity **Console**.

Then, follow these steps:

1. Go back to Unity and have the **Console** panel showing
2. Now click **Play**

Oh no! Nothing happened! Hold on... Actually, as you sit there looking at the blank **Console** panel, the script is running perfectly, just as we programmed it. The first part of line **16** in the script is waiting for you to press the *Enter* key. Press it now.

And there you go! The following screenshot shows you the result of adding two variables that contain the numbers **2** and **9**:

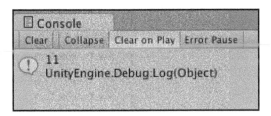

In our `LearningScript`, line **16** waited for you to press the *Enter* key. When you do this, the `AddTwoNumbers()` method is executed. When you do this, line **17**, which calls the `AddTwoNumbers()` method, is executed. This allows the code block of the method, line **23**, to add the values stored in the `number1` and `number2` variables.

While Unity is in the **Play** mode, select **Main Camera** so that its components appear in the **Inspector** panel. In the **Inspector** panel, locate `variableScript` and its two variables. Change the values, currently `2` and `9`, to something else. Make sure that you click on the **Game** panel so that it has focus. Then press the *Enter* key again. You will see the result of the new addition in **Console**.

You just learned how a method works to allow a specific block of code to be called in order to perform a task. We didn't get into any of the wording details of methods here. This was just to show you fundamentally how they work. We'll get into the finer details of methods in a later chapter.

Introducing the class

The class plays a major role in Unity. Most of your code will be written inside classes. Think of it like a container for variables and methods.

You just learned about variables and methods. These two items are the building blocks used in Unity scripts. The term "script" is used everywhere in discussions and documents. Look for it in the dictionary, and you will see that it can generally be described as written text. Sure enough, that's what we have. However, since we aren't just writing a screenplay or passing a note to someone, we need to learn the actual terms used in programming.

Unity calls the code it creates a C# script. However, people like me have to teach you some basic programming skills and tell you that a script is really a class.

In the previous section about methods, we created a class (script) called `variableScript`. It contained a couple of variables and a method. The main concept, or idea, of a class is that it's a container of data, stored in variables and methods that process that data in some fashion. Because I don't have to constantly write class (script), I will be using the word "script" most of the time. However, I will also be using "class" when getting more specific with C#. Just remember that a script is a class that is attached to a `GameObject`.

A script is like a blueprint or a written description. In other words, it's just a single file in a folder on our hard drive. We can see it right there in the **Projects** panel. It can't do anything by just sitting there. When we tell Unity to attach it to a `GameObject`, we aren't creating another copy of the file. All we're doing is telling Unity that we want the behaviors described in our script to be a component of the `GameObject`.

When we click the **Play** button, Unity loads the `GameObject` into the computer's memory. Since the script is attached to a `GameObject`, Unity also has to make a place in the computer's memory to store a component as part of the `GameObject`. The component has the capabilities specified in the script (blueprint) that we created.

It is worth knowing that not every class is a Unity component. In object–oriented programming, we use classes to organize the project. The last thing I want to do is get you confused at this stage, so it's a good idea here to write some code examples. Don't worry about writing it in your **MonoDevelop**. Just look at the examples and try to understand what classes might be used for.

- **Example 1 – Student**:

```
using UnityEngine;
using System.Collections;

public class Person : MonoBehaviour {

    public string firstName = "Greg";
    public string lastName = "Lukosek";
    public string emailAddress = "lukos86@gmail.com";
    public int age = 28;
    public float heightInMeters = 1.75f;

}
```

- **Example 2 – Car**:

```
using UnityEngine;
using System.Collections;

public class Car : MonoBehaviour {

    public string make = "Tesla"
    public string model = "S";
    public int numberOfWheels = 4;
    public int topSpeed = 250;


}
```

Inheritance

Unity components inherit from `MonoBehaviour` and that is what makes the code that we are creating work inside Unity and not in other C# applications. For beginners to Unity, studying C# inheritance isn't a subject you need to learn in any great detail, but you do need to know that each Unity script uses inheritance. We see the code in every script that will be attached to a `GameObject`. In `variableScript`, the code is on line **4**:

```
public class variableScript : MonoBehaviour
```

The colon and the last word of this code mean that the `variableScript` class is inheriting behaviors from the `MonoBehaviour` class. This simply means that the `MonoBehaviour` class is making a few of its variables and methods available to the `variableScript` class. It's no coincidence that the variables and methods inherited look like some of the code that we saw in the Unity **Scripting Reference**.

The following are the two inherited behaviors in the `variableScript` class:

```
Line 10: void Start ()
Line 15: void Update ()
```

You don't have to call these methods; Unity calls them *behind the scenes*. So, the code that you place in these methods gets executed automatically.

The Start(), Update(), and Awake() methods, and the execution order

The Start(), Update(), and Awake() methods are called automatically. The Start() method is called on the frame when the script is enabled. For most of our components, this will be when you press the **Start** button in Unity.

The Awake() method is called just before the Start() method. That gives a very convenient place to set up code if you have any. The Update() method is very specific. It's called on every frame if the component is enabled. It's very useful for observing user keyboard actions, for example. As you can see in our script, in Line **16** we are checking on every frame to find out whether the user has pressed the *Enter* key.

Let's create a new C# script and call it LearningMethods. As you can see, the Start() and Update() methods are added automatically when you create a new script. To test them all, all that we need to do is add the Awake() method and a few other useful lines to print something on the **Console** panel:

```
1   using UnityEngine;
2   using System.Collections;
3
4   public class LearningMethods : MonoBehaviour {
5
6
7       void Awake() {
8           Debug.Log("Awake function is called");
9       }
10
11      // Use this for initialization
12      void Start () {
13          Debug.Log("Start function is called");
14      }
15
16      // Update is called once per frame
17      void Update () {
18          Debug.Log("Update function is called");
19      }
20  }
21
22
23
```

As you already know, our three methods should be called in a very specific order. Add the `LearningMethods` component to some `GameObject` in the Unity scene and press **Play**. Then stop after two seconds. Keep an eye on the **Console** tab:

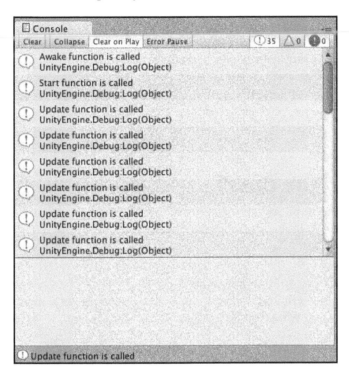

Wow! A lot of stuff on the **Console** tab? Why? Scroll up to the very top of the **Console** list. We can observe that Unity has printed the **Debug:Log** information from our `Awake()` method, followed by the `Start()` method. Then the madness starts. Unity prints tons of messages from the `Update()` method. We know why! `Update()` is called on every frame, so Unity will execute the lines of code within `Update()` forever, for every frame it renders.

You can, of course, print other information to **Console**–not just messages. Replace line **18** with this line:

```
Debug.Log(Time.time);
```

Press **Play** in Unity. You will notice that the time, in seconds, is printed, after you have pressed the **Play** button. It's fun, isn't it? Maybe not. Don't worry, we will get into much more interesting programming after we cover dot syntax.

Components that communicate using dot syntax

Our script has variables for holding data, and our script has methods to allow tasks to be performed. I now want to introduce the concept of communicating with other GameObjects and the components they contain. Communication between one component's GameObject and another component's GameObject using dot syntax is a vital part of scripting. It's what makes interaction possible. We need to communicate with other components or GameObjects to be able to use the variables and methods in other components.

What's with the dots?

When you look at code written by others, you'll see words with periods separating them. What the heck is that? It looks complicated, doesn't it? The following is an example from the Unity documentation:

```
transform.position.x
```

 Don't concern yourself with what the preceding code means, as that comes later. I just want you to see the dots.

This is called dot syntax. The following is another example. It's the fictitious address of my house: UnitedKingdom, Bedfordshire, Sandy, 10MyStreet. Looks funny, doesn't it? That's because I used the syntax (grammar) of C# instead of the post office. However, I'll bet that if you look closely, you can easily figure out how to find my house. We'll get into much more at a later stage. For now, think of dot syntax as an address, starting from a big thing, a country in this case, and narrowing down to the most precise part that we want to access.

Making decisions in code

The fundamental mechanism of programming is making decisions. In everyday life, we make hundreds and possibly thousands of decisions a day. They might be the results of simple questions such as "Do I need an umbrella today?" or "Should I drive at the maximum highway speed at the moment?" Let's first take a question and draw a single graph, as follows:

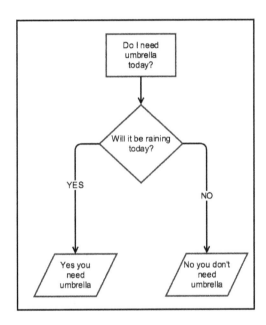

This is a fairly easy question. If it will be raining, I will need an umbrella; otherwise, I won't. In programming, we call it an `if` statement. It's a way we describe to the computer what code should be executed under what conditions. The question "Will it be raining?" is the condition. When planning your code, you should always break decision–making down into simple questions that can be answered only by a "yes" or a "no."

In C# syntax, we use `true` or `false` instead of yes or no.

We now know how the simplest `if` statements work. Let's see how this question will look in code. Let's create a new script, name it `LearningStatements`, and add it to a `GameObject` in the scene:

```
1 □ using UnityEngine;
2 └ using System.Collections;
3
4 □ public class LearningStatements : MonoBehaviour {
5
6        public bool willItBeRainingToday = true;
7
8 □     void Start () {
9
10           if (willItBeRainingToday) {
11               Debug.Log("Yes you need umbrella");
12           } else {
13               Debug.Log("No, you dont need umbrella");
14           }
15       }
16 └ }
17
```

Look at the code on line **10** and its description:

```
if (willItBeRainingToday)
```

An `if` statement is used to test whether the condition between the parentheses is true or false. The `willItBeRainingToday` variable stores a value `true`. Therefore, the code block in line **11** will be executed. Go ahead and hit **Play** in the **Editor** tab. The **Console** will print outline **11**.

Line **12** contains the `else` keyword. Everything within the brackets after the `else` keyword is executed only if the previous conditions aren't met. To test how it works, we press **Stop** in the editor, and on the `GameObject` containing our `LearningStatements` script, we change our variable value by ticking the checkbox in the **Inspector** panel. Then press **Play** again.

Using the NOT operator to change the condition

Here's a little curveball to wrap your mind around: the `NOT` logical operator. It's written in code using an exclamation mark. This makes a true condition false, or a false condition true. Let's add a `NOT` operator to our statement. Line **10** should now look like this:

```
if ( ! willItBeRainingToday ) {
```

Press **Play** in the editor. You will notice that the decision1;making is now working the opposite way. Line **11** will be executed only if the `willItBeRaining` variable is false.

Checking many conditions in an if statement

Sometimes, you will want your `if` statements to check many conditions before any code block is executed. This is very easy to do. There are two more logical operators that you can use:

- **AND**: This is used by putting `&&` between the conditions being checked. The code inside the curly brackets is executed only if all the conditions are true:

```
6       public bool imLateForMeeting = true;
7       public bool roadConditionsArePerfect = true;
8
9       void Start () {
10
11          if (imLateForMeeting && roadConditionsArePerfect) {
12              Debug.Log("I need to drive fast");
13          }
14      }
```

- **OR**: This is used by putting `||` between the conditions being checked. Then, the code inside the curly brackets is executed if any of the conditions are true:

```
16
17      public bool imHugry = false;
18      public bool areKidsHungry = true;
19
20      void Start () {
21
22          if (imHugry || areKidsHungry) {
23              Debug.Log("I should cook some food");
24          }
25      }
26
```

Using else if to make complex decisions

So far, we have learned how to decide what code we want to execute if certain conditions are met. Using `if` and `else`, we can decide what code is executed out of two parts. You are probably wondering, "What if I have many more complex decisions to make and need to be able to choose between more than two code blocks?" Yes, good question!

The `else if` expression is an expression that you can add after the code block belonging to the first `if` statement. Don't worry, it's not complicated. Let's take another example. Imagine you are driving a car and you need to check the speed limit and decide what speed you want to drive at:

```
 7 □    void Start () {
 8
 9            int speedLimit = 60;
10
11            if (speedLimit == 70) {
12                Debug.Log("I can drive at maximum speed");
13            }
14            else if (speedLimit < 70 && speedLimit >= 30) {
15                Debug.Log("Speed limit is less than 70 and more or equals to 30");
16            }
17            else if (speedLimit < 30) {
18                Debug.Log("I better be driving slowly, 30 mph or less");
19            }
20        }
21
22
```

Let's analyze the code:

- **Line 9**: This line declares the `speedLimit` number variable and assigns a value of `60`.
- **Line 11**: The `if` statement checks whether the `speedLimit` variable is exactly `70`. As we have assigned `speedLimit` as `60`, the statement in line **11** is false, so line **12** won't be executed.
- **Line 14**: The compiler will check this statement whenever the statement directly before `else` is false. Don't panic, it sounds very confusing now. All you need to know at the moment is that the `else if` statement is checked only if the previous statement isn't true.
- **Line 17**: Analogically, line **17** is checked only if line **14** is false.

 Of course, you can nest `if` statements inside each other. The syntax would look exactly the same. Simply write your new *child* `if` statement between the curly brackets of the *parent* statement.

Making decisions based on user input

Decisions always have to be made when the user provides input. The input can arrive from different types of interfaces depending on the platform that we are working on. For example, if we are developing games for mobile phones, we would use the touch screen as an input for swipe, touch, touch with two fingers, and so on, while for game consoles we would use the gamepad buttons. For each button, we can assign an action and it's possible to combine multiple buttons (inputs) to perform different actions. Another important aspect that we need to consider is that when we press a key or a button, three different inputs are happening at that instance, **GetKey**, **GetKeyDown**, and **GetKeyUp**:

GetKey	Returns true while the user holds down the key identified by name. Think auto fire.
GetKeyDown	Returns true during the frame the user starts pressing down the key identified by name.
GetKeyUp	Returns true during the frame the user releases the key identified by name.

As we can see in the preceding description, we can assign three different actions for the same key, so we are not limited to only one option. Previously in this chapter, we used an example where the user had to press the *Enter* key to call the AddTwoNumbers() method:

```
if(Input.GetKeyUp(Keycode.Return)) AddTwoNumbers();
```

The if statement's condition becomes true only when the *Return* key is released after being pressed down.

 Notice that the code of AddTwoNumbers() isn't between two curly brackets. When there is only one line of code to execute for an if or else statement, you have the option of not using the curly brackets.

Here's a partial screenshot of the `GetKeyUp()` method, as shown in Unity's **Scripting Reference**:

<u>**Input**</u>**.GetKeyUp**

public static bool **GetKeyUp**(string **name**);

Parameters

Description

Returns true during the frame the user releases the key identified by name.

Pencil and paper are powerful tools

We went through a few simple examples. For us humans, it's fairly simple to comprehend a few variables, `if` statements, and methods. Imagine, however, that you need to write a game containing many thousands of lines of code. It is very easy to get lost in your own project, trust me! There are many good practices and tools that can help you keep your project manageable. The most powerful one is planning. Plan as much as you can, write down ideas, and make notes. Draw flowcharts to break down complex decisions and you will be fine!

Summary

This chapter introduced the basic concepts of variables, methods, and the dot syntax. These building blocks are used to create scripts and classes. Understanding how these building blocks work is critical, so you don't feel you're not getting it.

We discovered that a variable name is a substitute for the value it stores, a method name is a substitute for a block of code, and when a script or class is attached to a `GameObject`, it becomes a component. The dot syntax is just like an address for locating `GameObjects` and components.

You also learned how to make decisions in code based on variable values. With these concepts under your belt, you can proceed to learn the details of the sentence structure, grammar, and syntax used to work with variables, methods, and the dot syntax. In the next chapter, we will cover the details of using variables.

3
Getting into the Details of Variables

Initially, computer programming appears difficult to beginners due to the way in which words are used in code. It's not the actual words that cause the problem because, for most of the part, many of the words are the same as those we use in our everyday life. C# is not a foreign language. The main problem is that the words simply don't read like the typical sentences that we are all used to. You know how to say words and how to spell words. What you don't know is where and why you need to put them in that crazy-looking grammar, that is, the syntax that makes up a C# statement.

In this chapter, you will learn some of the basic rules of writing a C# statement. We will also introduce many of the words that C# uses and the proper placement of these words in C# statements when we create our variables.

In this chapter, we will cover the following topics:

- Writing C# statements properly
- Using C# syntax to write variable statements
- The GameObject component's properties
- Using public variables for the Unity **Inspector** panel
- Naming a variable properly
- Declaring a variable for the type of data it will store

Writing C# statements properly

When you do normal writing, it's in the form of a sentence, with a period used to end the sentence. When you write a line of code, it's called a statement, with a semicolon used to end the statement. This is necessary because the console reads the code one line at a time and it's necessary to use a semicolon to tell the console that the line of code is over and that the console can jump to the next line. (This is happening so fast that it looks like the computer is reading all of them at the same time, but it isn't.) When we start learning how to code, forgetting about this detail is very common, so don't forget to check for this error if the code isn't working:

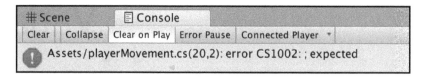

 The reason a statement ends with a semicolon is so that Unity knows when the statement ends. A period can't be used because it is used in the dot syntax.

The code for a C# statement does not have to be on a single line as shown in the following example:

```
public int number1 = 2;
```

The statement can be on several lines. Whitespace and carriage returns are ignored, so, if you really want to, you can write it as follows:

```
public
int
number1
=
2;
```

However, I do not recommend writing your code like this because it's terrible to read code that is formatted like the preceding code. Nevertheless, there will be times when you'll have to write long statements that are longer than one line. Unity won't care. It just needs to see the semicolon at the end.

Understanding component properties in Unity's Inspector

GameObjects have some components that make them behave in a certain way. For instance, select **Main Camera** and look at the Inspector panel. One of the components is the camera. Without that component, it will cease being a camera. It would still be a GameObject in your scene, just no longer a functioning camera.

Variables become component properties

When we refer to components, we are basically referring to the available functions of a GameObject, for example, the human body has many functions, such as talking, moving, and observing. Now let's say that we want the human body to move faster. What is the function linked to that action? Movement. So in order to make our body move faster, we would need to create a script that had access to the movement component and then we would use that to make the body move faster. Just like in real life, different GameObjects can also have different components, for example, the camera component can only be accessed from a camera. There are plenty of components that already exist that were created by Unity's programmers, but we can also write our own components. This means that all the properties that we see in **Inspector** are just variables of some type. They simply store data that will be used by some method.

Unity changes script and variable names slightly

When we create a script, one of the first things that we need to do is give a name to the script and it's always good practice to use a name that identifies the content of the script. For example, if we are creating a script that is used to control the player movement, ideally that would be the name of the script. The best practice is to write `playerMovement`, where the first word is uncapitalized and the second one is capitalized. This is the standard way Unity developers name scripts and variables. Now let's say that we created a script named `playerMovement`. After assigning that script to a GameObject, we'll see that in the **Inspector** panel we would see that Unity adds a space to separate the words of the name, Player Movement. Unity does this modification to variable names too where, for example, a variable named `number1` is shown as **Number 1** and `number2` as **Number 2**. Unity capitalizes the first letter as well. These changes improve readability in **Inspector**.

Changing a property's value in the Inspector panel

There are two situations where you can modify a property value:

- During the **Play** mode
- During the development stage (not in the **Play** mode)

When you are in the **Play** mode, you will see that your changes take effect immediately in real time. This is great when you're experimenting and want to see the results.

Write down any changes that you want to keep because when you stop the **Play** mode, any changes you made will be lost.

When you are in the **Development** mode, changes that you make to the property values will be saved by Unity. This means that if you quit Unity and start it again, the changes will be retained. Of course, you won't see the effect of your changes until you click **Play**.

The changes that you make to the property values in the **Inspector** panel do not modify your script. The only way your script can be changed is by you editing it in the script editor (MonoDevelop). The values shown in the **Inspector** panel override any values you might have assigned in your script.

If you want to undo the changes you've made in the **Inspector** panel, you can reset the values to the default values assigned in your script. Click on the cog icon (the gear) on the far right of the component script, and then select **Reset**, as shown in the following screenshot:

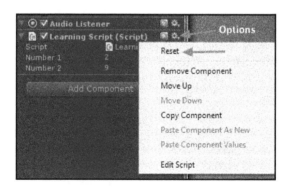

Displaying public variables in the Inspector panel

You might still be wondering what the word `public` at the beginning of a variable statement means:

```
public int number1 = 2;
```

We mentioned it before. It means that the variable will be visible and accessible. It will be visible as a property in the **Inspector** panel so that you can manipulate the value stored in the variable. The word also means that it can be accessed from other scripts using the dot syntax.

Private variables

Not all variables need to be public. If there's no need for a variable to be changed in the **Inspector** panel or be accessed from other scripts, it doesn't make sense to clutter the **Inspector** panel with needless properties. In the `LearningScript`, perform the following steps:

1. Change line **6** to this:

   ```
   private int number1 = 2;
   ```

2. Then change line **7** to the following:

   ```
   int number2 = 9;
   ```

3. Save the file
4. In Unity, select **Main Camera**

You will notice in the **Inspector** panel that both properties, **Number 1** and **Number 2**, are gone:

```
Line 6: private int number1 = 2;
```

The preceding line explicitly states that the `number1` variable has to be private. Therefore, the variable is no longer a property in the **Inspector** panel. It is now a private variable for storing data:

```
Line 7: int number2 = 9;
```

The `number2` variable is no longer visible as a property either, but you didn't specify it as `private`. If you don't explicitly state whether a variable will be public or private, by default, the variable will implicitly be private in C#.

It is good coding practice to explicitly state whether a variable will be public or private.

So now, when you click **Play**, the script works exactly as it did before. You just can't manipulate the values manually in the **Inspector** panel anymore.

Naming your variables properly

As we explored previously, naming a script or variable is a very important step. It won't change the way that the code runs, but it will help us to stay organized and, by using best practices, we are avoiding errors and saving time trying to find the piece of code that isn't working. Always use meaningful names to store your variables. If you don't do that, six months down the line, you will be lost. I'm going to exaggerate here a bit to make a point. Let's say you will name a variable as shown in this code:

```
public bool areRoadConditionsPerfect = true;
```

That's a descriptive name. In other words, you know what it means by just reading the variable. So 10 years from now, when you look at that name, you'll know exactly what I meant in the previous comment. Now suppose that instead of `areRoadConditionsPerfect`, you had named this variable as shown in the following code:

```
public bool perfect = true;
```

Sure, you know what perfect is, but would you know that it refers to perfect road conditions? I know that right now you'll understand it because you just wrote it, but six months down the line, after writing hundreds of other scripts for all sorts of different projects, you'll look at this word and wonder what you meant. You'll have to read several lines of code you wrote to try to figure it out.

You may look at the code and wonder who in their right mind would write such terrible code. So, take your time to write descriptive code that even a stranger can look at and know what you mean. Believe me, in six months or probably less time, you will be that stranger.

 Using meaningful names for variables and methods is helpful not only for you but also for any other game developer who will be reading your code. Whether or not you work in a team, you should always write easy-to-read code.

Beginning variable names with lowercase

You should begin a variable name with a lowercase letter because it helps distinguish between a class name and a variable name in your code. There are some other guides in the C# documentation as well, but we don't need to worry about them at this stage. Component names (class names) begin with an uppercase letter. For example, it's easy to know that `Transform` is a class and `transform` is a variable.

There are, of course, exceptions to this general rule, and every programmer has a preferred way of using lowercase, uppercase, and perhaps an underscore to begin a variable name. In the end, you will have to decide upon a naming convention that you like. If you read the Unity forums, you will notice that there are some heated debates on naming variables. In this book, I will show you my preferred way, but you can use whatever is more comfortable for you.

Using multiword variable names

Let's use the same example again, as follows:

```
public bool areRoadConditionsPerfect = true;
```

You can see that the variable name is actually four words squeezed together. Since variable names can be only one word, begin the first word with a lowercase and then just capitalize the first letter of every additional word. This greatly helps create descriptive names that the viewer is still able to read. There's a term for this, it's called **camel casing**.

I have already mentioned that for public variables, Unity's **Inspector** will separate each word and capitalize the first word. Go ahead! Add the previous statement to the `LearningScript` and see what Unity does with it in the **Inspector** panel.

Declaring a variable and its type

Every variable that we want to use in a script must be declared in a statement. What does that mean? Well, before Unity can use a variable, we have to tell Unity about it first. Okay then, what are we supposed to tell Unity about the variable?

There are only three absolute requirements to declare a variable and they are as follows:

- We have to specify the type of data that a variable can store
- We have to provide a name for the variable
- We have to end the declaration statement with a semicolon

The following is the syntax we use to declare a variable:

```
typeOfData nameOfTheVariable;
```

Let's use one of the `LearningScript` variables as an example; the following is how we declare a variable with the bare minimum requirements:

```
int number1;
```

This is what we have:

- **Requirement #1** is the type of data that `number1` can store, which in this case is an `int`, meaning an integer
- **Requirement #2** is a name, which is `number1`
- **Requirement #3** is the semicolon at the end

The second requirement of naming a variable has already been discussed. The third requirement of ending a statement with a semicolon has also been discussed. The first requirement of specifying the type of data will be covered next.

The following is what we know about this bare minimum declaration as far as Unity is concerned:

- There's no public modifier, which means it's private by default
- It won't appear in the **Inspector** panel or be accessible from other scripts
- The value stored in `number1` defaults to zero

The most common built-in variable types

This section shows only the most common built-in types of data that C# provides for us and that the variables can store.

Only the basic types are presented here so that you understand the concept of a variable being able to store only the type of the data that you specify. Custom types of data, which you will create later, will be discussed in Chapter 7, *Object, Container with Variables and Methods*.

The following chart shows the most common built-in types of data you will use in Unity:

Type	Contents of the variable
int	A simple integer, such as the number 3
float	A number with a decimal, such as the number 3.14
string	Characters in double quotes, such as, "Watch me go now"
bool	A boolean, either **true** or **false**

 There are a few more built-in types of data that aren't shown in the preceding chart. However, once you understand the most common types, you'll have no problem looking up the other built-in types if you ever need to use them. You can also create your own classes and store their instances in variables.

We know the minimum requirements to declare a variable. However, we can add more information to a declaration to save time and coding. In the `LearningScript`, we've already seen some examples of assigning values when the variable is being declared, and now we'll see some more examples.

Assigning values while declaring a variable

When we create a variable, there are two ways to access and edit the values, either by code or by the Unity **Inspector** panel. Editing the values by code means that the values are dynamic, they can be changed at any time, they can be updated at the start of the script, or at any other time. If we choose to edit the variables in the Unity **Inspector** panel, we are assuming that the values will remain the same throughout the game.

Let's create a new script and test this:

```
 1 using System.Collections;
 2 using System.Collections.Generic;
 3 using UnityEngine;
 4
 5 public class playerMovement : MonoBehaviour {
 6
 7     public int minSpeed = 5;
 8     public int maxSpeed = 10;
 9     public int averageSpeed;
10
11     // Use this for initialization
12     void Start () {
13
14     }
15
16     // Update is called once per frame
17     void Update () {
18
19     }
20 }
21
```

We have created a few variables, one for the minimum speed, max speed and average speed. The idea now is to calculate the average speed, this means that this value will be dynamic while the other two will be static. So on `void Update()`, we'll write a simple line of code to calculate the average speed, `averageSpeed = (minSpeed + maxSpeed) / 2;`:

```
// Update is called once per frame
void Update () {

    averageSpeed = (minSpeed + maxSpeed) / 2;
}
```

Now we assign this script to the `GameObject` camera to test it (drag and drop the script over the camera `GameObject`). By doing this, we are now able to edit the min and max values on the Unity `Inspector` panel, we can do this before clicking the **Play** button or at any time after that, but remember that this (updating the values in the middle of the game) is only available to do on the Unity program for test proposes:

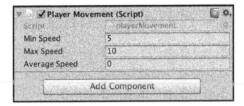

As we can see, the value for the average speed will be zero until we click **Play**:

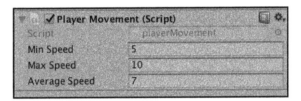

After clicking the play button, the average speed value starts working and we can test this by assigning different values for the min and max speed.

The variables are displayed in the **Inspector** panel with the values set by default in the code. Remember that from now on, the value in the **Inspector** panel will override the value in the code, so if you decide to change your code a little, the value in **Inspector** will stay as it was initially.

Where you declare a variable is important

So far, we have learned how to create variables and we have written all of them at the beginning of the script. This is where most of the variables will be written, but it's not the only place where we can write them. You will be declaring and using variables in many places in a script. The variables that I have shown you so far are called member variables. These member variables are the only variables that have the option of being displayed in the **Inspector** panel or being accessed by other scripts.

 Declaring your member variables at the beginning of a class may give you a mental clue that these member variables can be used anywhere in the script.

We will also be creating variables in methods. These variables are called local variables. They are never displayed in the Unity's **Inspector** panel, nor can they be accessed by other scripts. This brings us to another concept of programming, called variable scope.

Variable scope - determining where a variable can be used

Variable scope is a fancy way of saying, "Where in the script a variable exists." The following screenshot explains the scope of some variables:

```
1  using UnityEngine;
2  using System.Collections;
3
4  public class LearningScript : MonoBehaviour
5  {
6      string block1 = "Block 1 text";          Code Block 1
7
8      void Start ()
9      {
10         Debug.Log(block1);                    Code Block 2
11         string block2 = "Block 2 text";
12         Debug.Log(block2);
13         {
14             Debug.Log(block1);                Code Block 3
15             Debug.Log(block2);
16             string block3 = "Block 3 text";
17             Debug.Log(block3);
18         }
19     }
20  }
```

You might have noticed that the rectangular blocks start and end with curly brackets. Just like the AddTwoNumbers() method in Chapter 2, *Introducing the Building Blocks for Unity Scripts*, the code between an opening curly bracket and a closing curly bracket is called a code block. Absolutely wherever in a code you have an opening curly bracket, there will be a closing curly bracket to match. All of the code between the two brackets is a code block. Notice that code blocks can be nested inside other code blocks.

 You normally won't create bare blocks of code with curly brackets like I did in the case of **Code Block 3**. Code blocks usually include other things, such as if statements, looping statements, and methods. This example is just to demonstrate how the scope of a variable works and where a variable exists and is usable.

The following is what you have:

```
Line 16: string block3 = "Block 3 text";
```

The preceding line declares a local string variable named `block3`. This variable exists in the code block that is labeled **Code Block 3**. If you try to use the `block3` variable outside of **Code Block 3**, such as in **Code Block 2** or **Code Block 1**, Unity will give you an error message saying that the `block3` variable doesn't exist.

The scope of the `block3` variable is the code block defined by the curly brackets of lines **13** and **18**:

```
Line 6: string block1 = "Block 1 text";
```

The preceding line declares a string type member variable named `block1`. This variable exists in the code block that is labeled **Code Block 1**. This code block begins on line **5** and ends on line **20**. This means that the `block1` variable can be used everywhere, including **Code Block 2** and **Code Block 3**, because they are also within **Code Block 1**. The `block1` variable is used in **Code Block 2** on line **10** and in **Code Block 3** on line **14**.

Thus, the scope of the `block1` variable is the code block defined by the curly brackets between lines **5** and **20**.

Summary

First, we covered how to write a C# statement, especially the semicolon for terminating a statement. All the component properties shown in the **Inspector** panel are member variables in the component's class. Member variables can be shown in the **Inspector** panel or accessed by other scripts when the variable is declared public. The type of data that a variable can store is specified when it's declared. Finally, you learned that variable scope determines where it is allowed to be used.

Now that you've learned about variables, you're ready to learn the details of the C# methods that will use the variables we create, which is the topic of the next chapter.

4
Getting into the Details of Methods

In the previous chapter, you were introduced to a variable's scope, within which a variable exists and is allowed to be used. The scope is determined by the *opening* and *closing* curly brackets. The purpose of those curly brackets is to act as a container for a block of executable code, a code block. In the second chapter, you understood that a method is a code block that can execute by just calling the method's name. It's time to understand the importance of code blocks and the variables used in them. A method defines a code block that begins and ends with curly brackets.

In this chapter, we will cover the following topics:

- Using methods in a script
- Naming methods the good way
- Defining a method
- Calling a method
- Returning a value from a method

Variables are the first major building block of C# and methods are the second, so let's dive into methods.

Using methods in a script

There are two reasons to use methods in a script:

- To provide a behavior to GameObject
- To create reusable sections of code

All of the executable code in a script is inside methods. The first purpose of a method is to work with the member variables of the class. The member variables store data that is needed for a component to give a GameObject its behavior. The whole reason for writing a script is to make a GameObject do something interesting. A method is a place where we make a behavior come to life.

The second purpose of a method is to create code blocks that will be used over and over again. You don't want to be writing the same code over and over. Instead, you place the code in a code block and give it a name so that you can call it whenever needed.

Let's take a quick look at this example:

```
void AddAndPrintTwoNumbers(int number1, int number2) {

    int result = number1 + number2;
    Debug.Log(result);

}
```

This is a perfect example of the function that does something useful. It might look a bit strange to you as it takes two parameters. Don't worry about it too much for now, we will cover it in detail soon. All I want you to notice right now is that the preceding method can take some data and do something useful with it. In this case, it is adding two numbers and printing the result on the Unity console. Now, the best part: we can call this method as many times as we want, passing different parameters, without repeating the code every time we need it. If you feel confused, don't worry. Just remember that a function can save you from repeating code over and over again.

Methods can also return some data. We will cover this at a later stage in this chapter.

Naming methods properly

Always use meaningful names for your methods. Just as I explained for variables, if you don't use good names, then six months from now, you will be confused.

Since methods make the `GameObject` do something useful, you should give your method a name that sounds like an *action*, for example, `JumpOverTheFence` or `ClimbTheWall`. You can look at those names and know exactly what the method is going to do.

Don't make them too simple. Suppose you name a method `Wiggle`. Sure, you know what `Wiggle` means right now, but six months later, you'll look at that and say "Wiggle? Wiggle what?" It takes only a moment more to be a little more precise and write `WiggleDogsTail`. Now, when you see this method name, you'll know exactly what it's going to do.

Beginning method names with an uppercase letter

Why? We do this to make it easier to tell the difference between a class or method and a variable. Also, Microsoft recommends beginning method names with an uppercase letter. If someone else ever looks at your code, they will expect to see method names beginning with an uppercase letter.

Using multiword names for a method

Let's use this example again:

```
void AddTwoNumbers ()
{
  // Code goes here
}
```

You can see that the name is actually three words squished together. Since method names can have only one word, the first word begins with an uppercase, and then we just capitalize the first letter of every additional word, for example, `PascalCasing`.

Parentheses are part of the method's name

The method name always includes a pair of parentheses at the end. These parentheses not only let you know that the name is of a method but also serve the important purpose of allowing you to input some data into the method when needed.

Defining a method the right way

Just as with variables, we have to let Unity know about a method before we can use it. Depending on who you talk to, some will say, "We have to declare a method," others will say, "We have to define a method," or even, "We have to implement a method." Which is correct? In C#, it doesn't make any difference. Use whichever term helps you learn more easily. I like to say I'm defining a method's code block, nothing like declaring a simple variable on a one-line statement.

The minimum requirements for defining a method

There are three minimum requirements for defining a method:

- The type of information, or data, that a method will return to the place from where it was called
- The name of the method should be followed by a pair of parentheses
- A pair of curly braces should be present to contain the code block:

```
returnDataType  NameOfTheMethod ( )
{

}
```

At this point, we already know that when we create a new script, there are two methods that always appear by default, `Start()` and `Update()`. We can see that the `Start()` and `Update()` methods have the three minimum requirements for a method:

```
void Start ()
{

}

void Update ()
```

```
{

}
```

Here's what we have:

- Our first requirement is the type of data that the method will return to the place in the code that called this method. This method isn't returning any value, so instead of specifying an actual type of data, the `void` keyword is used. This informs Unity that nothing is being returned from the method.
- The second requirement is the method name, which is `Start()`.
- The last requirement is the curly brackets, `{ }`. They contain the code that defines what the method is going to do.

This example fulfills the bare minimum requirements for a method. However, as you can see, there's no code in the code block, so when `Start()` is called by Unity, it doesn't do anything at all. Yet, it's a method. Normally, if we aren't going to use a method by adding code to a skeleton method created by Unity, we can simply remove it from our script. It's normally best to remove unused code after the script has been written.

Here's what we know about this bare-minimum method definition as far as Unity is concerned:

- There's no public modifier, which means that this method is private by default. Therefore, this method cannot be called from other scripts.
- There's no code in the code block. Therefore, this method doesn't do anything. So, it can be removed if we want to remove it.

Most of the code that we are going to write will be inside of these two methods `Start()` and `Update()`, but we need to keep in mind that we are able to create our own methods, allowing us to expand our capabilities even more, as we are going to explore in a moment.

 Methods that do not return any data use the `void` keyword instead of `datatype`.

Understanding parentheses - why are they there?

Parentheses definitely make it easy to recognize a method, but why are they part of a method's name?

We already know that a method is a code block that is going to be called multiple times. That's one of the reasons a method is created in the first place so that we don't have to write the same code over and over. Remember the `AddAndPrintTwoNumbers()` example method? We have mentioned that a method can take some input parameters. Why is this useful?

A script may need to add two numbers several times, but they probably won't always be the same two numbers. We can have possibly hundreds of different combinations of *two numbers* to add together. This means that we need to let the method know which two numbers need to be added together at the moment when we call the method. Let's write a code example to make sure you fully understand it:

```
1  using UnityEngine;
2  using System.Collections;
3
4  public class LearningReusableMethods : MonoBehaviour {
5
6
7      public int number1 = 2;
8      public int number2 = 3;
9      public int number3 = 7;
10
11
12
13     void Start () {
14
15         AddAndPrintTwoNumbers(number1, number2);
16         AddAndPrintTwoNumbers(number1, number3);
17         AddAndPrintTwoNumbers(number2, number3);
18
19     }
20
21
22
23     void AddAndPrintTwoNumbers(int firstNumber, int secondNumber) {
24
25         int result = firstNumber + secondNumber;
26         Debug.Log(result);
27
28     }
29
30
31
32  }
33
34
35
36
37
38
```

Lines **7**, **8**, and **9** should be quite clear to you as simple declarations of variables.

Let's take a look at the AddAndPrintTwoNumbers method. It's a void function. Again, this means the function does something but does not return any data. Inside the parentheses, our method takes two variables: firstNumber and secondNumber.

Line **25** contains the declaration and assignment of the local variable that we will be printing on line **26**.

So, AddAndPrintTwoNumbers is written the universal way. We can reuse this function as many times as we want, passing different parameters.

Lines **15**, **16**, and **17** call our function three times, each time passing different parameters to the function. Let's test whether it works! Go ahead, add the LearningReusableMethods component to any GameObject in the Unity scene, and click **Play**.

As this script executes, the AddAndPrintTwoNumbers method is called three times, on lines **15**, **16**, and **17**. The method's code block adds two numbers and displays the result in the Unity **Console** tab:

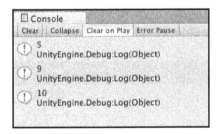

As expected! The console will print out the values. There's a special name for information between the parentheses of a method definition, such as line **23**: the code is called **method parameters**.

Specifying a method's parameters

If you look up the word "parameters" in the dictionary, your brain will probably seize up. All it means is that the method has to be able to use the information you send it, so you simply have to specify the type of data that the method is allowed to use. That's it! It's very simple.

In the earlier screenshot, on line **23**, we declared the `firstNumber` and `secondNumber` variables. The type is `int`. Now notice our member variables: `number1`, `number2`, and `number3`. They are also of the `int` type. These variables have to be of the `int` type since they store the numbers that will be added to the method, which the parameters specify will be of the `int` type.

So now, go look in the dictionary again. You will probably see the word limit in there somewhere. That's what you did when you specified the type of data that the method will use, an integer in this case. You set some limits on what is allowed.

Okay, so you're setting parameters, or limits, on the type of data the method can use, but what exactly is a parameter? Well, the first parameter is called `firstNumber`. And what is `firstNumber` doing? It stores a value that will be used in the code block on line **25**. What do we call things that store data? That's right, variables! Variables are used everywhere.

 Remember that a variable is just a substitute name for the value it actually stores.

As you can see on line **25** of the code block, those variables are being added and stored in the `result` variable.

How many parameters can a method have?

We can have as many parameters as we need to make a method work properly. Whether we write our own custom methods or use the methods of the scripting reference, the parameters that are defined are what the method will require to be able to perform its specified task.

Returning a value from a method

Now it's time to discover the *power* feature of using a method. This usually means sending data to the method, which you just learned to do. Then we have the method return a value. Previously, we used a `void` type method. I have mentioned before that this is a keyword for *nothing*, which means that the function isn't returning anything.

Let's learn about `return` type functions now. For this example, we won't use `void` anymore. Instead of that, we will write the type of data that we want our method to return. What is a return method? A return method is the result of all the code that we have written inside that method, it gives us an answer to the question that we choose to make. When should we use a return method? We can use this type of methods for multiple purposes, but almost all of them will have the same core functionality, solving a problem or answering a question. The return method will be there, ready to give us the answer at any time that we need; to do that, we just have to call that return method.

Let's take a look at the following example. I have highlighted two key areas that we will speak about next.

```
int AddTwoNumbers (int firstNumber, int secondNumber) {

    int result = firstNumber + secondNumber;
    return result;

}
```

As you can see, this method is very similar to the `AddAndPrintTwoNumbers` method that we spoke of previously. The two main differences are highlighted.

A `return` type function will always begin with a description of the type of data that it's returning. In this case, we will be returning the sum of two numbers, so our type is `int` (an integer). In simple words, the `AddTwoNumbers` function is returning a number.

Returning the value

Once you have decided what type of data will be returned by a method, you must tell the function what value will be returned. The syntax is very straightforward. We use the `return` keyword, highlighted in blue, followed by the value we are returning.

Example

You just learned how to write a `return` type method. Time to put it to use! Let's write a new script and call it `returnTotal`:

```
1 using System.Collections;
2 using UnityEngine;
3
4 public class returnTotal : MonoBehaviour {
5
6
7     public int number1 = 2;
8     public int number2 = 3;
9
10
11
12    void Start () {
13
14        int sumResult = AddTwoNumbers (number1, number2);
15
16        DisplayResult (sumResult);
17    }
18
19
20
21
22    int AddTwoNumbers (int firstNumber, int secondNumber) {
23
24        int result = firstNumber + secondNumber;
25        return result;
26
27    }
28
29
30    void DisplayResult (int total) {
31
32        Debug.Log("The grand total is : " + total);
33    }
34 }
35
36
37
38
39
40
```

What do we have here? You probably understand most of this code with no issues, but it's good practice to go through it line by line. Lines **7** and **8** contain declarations of the `number1` and `number2` integer variables. Lines **22** to **27** are exactly the same as we used in the last example. They have the declaration of a method that takes two parameters - `firstNumber` and `secondNumber` and it returns a value of the `int` type.

Lines **30** to **34** contain the declaration of the method that simply prints the given `int` value on the Unity console. In this case, it represents the sum of our two variables, `number1` and `number2`. Now is the most important part you need to remember. Take a look at line **14**:

```
int sumResult = AddTwoNumbers(number1, number2);
```

The left-hand side of this line is a simple declaration of an int variable called sumResult. Simple! What I want to talk about is the right-hand side-the assignment of this variable. As you can see, what we are doing here is calling the AddTwoNumbers method instead of simply giving the value to be stored in sumResult. It might look a bit awkward. You would expect a value to be passed instead of another method call.

Let me explain how it works. The AddTwoNumbers method is a return type method. It returns an int value in every place where you call it instantly. In even simpler words, AddTwoNumbers() is an integer and a number value.

This concept might be a bit difficult to get your head around. If you still don't get it, don't worry. All you need to remember right now is the fact that, whenever a program calls a method that returns something, it is calling the method and inserting the value that the method returns into the place where it made the call. Let's test this by calling this same method again to give us another result:

```
1 using System.Collections;
2 using UnityEngine;
3
4 public class returnTotal : MonoBehaviour {
5
6
7     public int number1 = 2;
8     public int number2 = 3;
9     public int number3 = 6;
10    public int number4 = 8;
11
12
13
14    void Start () {
15
16        int sumResult = AddTwoNumbers (number1, number2);
17        int sumAnotherResult = AddTwoNumbers (number3, number4);
18
19        DisplayResult (sumResult);
20        DisplayResult (sumAnotherResult);
21    }
22
23
24
25
26    int AddTwoNumbers (int firstNumber, int secondNumber) {
27
28        int result = firstNumber + secondNumber;
29        return result;
30    }
31
32
33    void DisplayResult (int total) {
34
35        Debug.Log("The grand total is : " + total);
36    }
37 }
38
39
40
```

So we added two new `int` variables called `number3` and `number4`, and inside the `Start()` method we updated the code to include a new sum result, `sumAnotherResult`. Now we have two different equations that we want to solve by using the `AddTwoNumbers` method which will return us the result for both equations separately and this is the result:

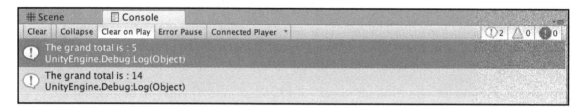

Remember I told you that, when you call a method, it's just a substitute for the code block that will be executed. It's like taking all of the code in the method's code block and placing it right where the method was called.

Summary

In this chapter, you learned more details about methods. We will start using methods everywhere in this book. Feel free to come back to this chapter if you feel lost.

In the next chapter, we will introduce the more complex ideas of handling, lists, arrays, and dictionaries.

5

Lists, Arrays, and Dictionaries

In previous chapters, you learned how to declare and use a single variable and its type. Now it's time for something more complex. As you know, we can store a value in a variable. But we can also store more than one value in a single variable. In this chapter, we will be talking about special types of variables that allow us to store many values at once.

In this chapter, we will cover the following topics:

- What arrays are and why it is good to use them
- Storing data in an array
- Retrieving data from an array
- Lists are powerful, using collections
- `List` or `ArrayList`
- An introduction to Dictionaries

What is an array?

An array stores a sequential collection of values of the same type, in the simplest terms. We can use arrays to store lists of values in a single variable. Imagine we want to store a number of student names. Simple! Just create a few variables and name them `student1`, `student2`, and so on:

```
public string student1 = "Greg";
public string student2 = "Kate";
public string student3 = "Adam";
public string student4 = "Mia";
```

There's nothing wrong with this. We can print and assign new values to them. The problem starts when you don't know how many student names you will be storing. The name variable suggests that it's a changing element. There is a much cleaner way of storing lists of data.

Let's store the same names using a C# array variable type:

```
public string[ ] familyMembers = new string[ ]{"Greg", "Kate", "Adam", "Mia"} ;
```

As you can see, all the preceding values are stored in a single variable called `familyMembers`.

Declaring an array

To declare a C# array, you must first say what type of data will be stored in the array. As you can see in the preceding example, we are storing strings of characters. After the type, we have an open square bracket and then immediately a closed square bracket, `[ ]`. This will make the variable an actual array. We also need to declare the size of the array. It simply means how many places are there in our variable to be accessed. The minimum code required to declare a variable looks similar to this:

```
public string[] myArrayName = new string[4];
```

The array size is set during assignment. As you have learned before, all code after the variable declaration and the equal sign is an assignment. To assign empty values to all places in the array, simply write the `new` keyword followed by the type, an open square bracket, a number describing the size of the array, and then a closed square bracket. If you feel confused, give yourself a bit more time. Then you will fully understand why arrays are helpful. Take a look at the following examples of arrays; don't worry about testing how they work yet:

```
string[ ] familyMembers = new string[]{"John", "Amanda", "Chris", "Amber"} ;

string[ ] carsInTheGarage = new string[] {"VWPassat", "BMW"} ;

int[ ] doorNumbersOnMyStreet = { 1, 2, 3, 4, 5, 6, 7, 8, 9, 10, 11, 12 };

GameObject[ ] carsInTheScene = GameObject.FindGameObjectsWithTag("car");
```

As you can see, we can store different types of data as long as the elements in the array are of the same type. You are probably wondering why the last example, shown here, looks different:

```
GameObject[ ] carsInTheScene = GameObject.FindGameObjectsWithTag("car");
```

In fact, we are just declaring the new array variable to store a collection of GameObject in the scene using the "car" tag. Jump into the Unity scripting documentation and search for GameObject.FindGameObjectsWithTag:

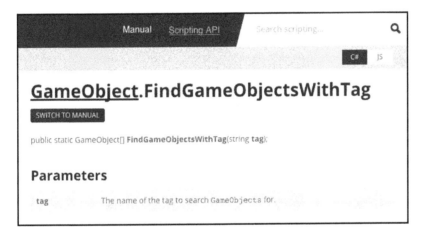

As you can see, GameObject.FindGameObjectsWithTag is a special built-in Unity function that takes a string parameter (tag) and returns an array of GameObjects using this tag.

Storing items in the List

Using a List instead of an array can be so easier to work with in a script. Look at some forum sites related to C# and Unity, and you'll discover that a great deal of programmers simply don't use an array unless they have to; they prefer to use a List. It is up to the developer's preference and task. Let's stick to lists for now.

Here are the basics of why a List is better and easier to use than an array:

- An array is of fixed size and unchangeable
- The size of a List is adjustable

- You can easily add and remove elements from a `List`
- To mimic adding a new element to an array, we would need to create a whole new array with the desired number of elements and then copy the old elements

The first thing to understand is that a `List` has the ability to store any type of object, just like an array. Also, like an array, we must specify which type of object we want a particular `List` to store. This means that if you want a List of integers of the `int` type then you can create a `List` that will store only the `int` type.

Let's go back to the first array example and store the same data in a List. To use a `List` in C#, you need to add the following line at the beginning of your script:

```
using System.Collections.Generic;
```

As you can see, using Lists is slightly different from using arrays. Line **9** is a declaration and assignment of the `familyMembers` List. When declaring the list, there is a requirement for a type of objects that you will be storing in the `List`. Simply write the type between the `< >` characters. In this case, we are using `string`.

As we are adding the actual elements later in lines **14** to **17**, instead of assigning elements in the declaration line, we need to assign an empty `List` to be stored temporarily in the `familyMembers` variable. Confused? If so, just take a look at the right-hand side of the equal sign on line **9**. This is how you create a new instance of the `List` for a given type, `string` for this example:

```
new List<string>();
```

```
1  using UnityEngine;
2  using System.Collections;
3  using System.Collections.Generic;
4
5
6  public class LearningLists : MonoBehaviour {
7
8
9      public List<string> familyMembers = new List<string>();
10
11
12      void Start() {
13
14          familyMembers.Add("Greg");
15          familyMembers.Add("Kate");
16          familyMembers.Add("Adam");
17          familyMembers.Add("Mia");
18
19      }
20
21  }
22
```

Lines **14** to **17** are very simple to understand. Each line adds an object at the end of the List, passing the string value in the parentheses.

 In various documentation, Lists of type look like this: List< T >. Here, T stands for the type of data. This simply means that you can insert any type in place of T and the List will become a list of that specific type. From now on, we will be using it.

Common operations with Lists

List<T> is very easy to use. There is a huge list of different operations that you can perform with it. We have already spoken about adding an element at the end of a List. Very briefly, let's look at the common ones that we will be possibly using at later stages:

- Add: This adds an object at the end of List<T>.
- Remove: This removes the first occurrence of a specific object from List<T>.
- Clear: This removes all elements from List<T>.
- Contains: This determines whether an element is in List<T> or not. It is very useful to check whether an element is stored in the list.
- Insert: This inserts an element into List<T> at the specified index.
- ToArray: This copies the elements of List<T> to a new array.

You don't need to understand all of these at this stage. All I want you to know is that there are many *out-of-the-box* operations that you can use. If you want to see them all, I encourage you to dive into the C# documentation and search for the List<T> class.

List <T> versus arrays

Now you are probably thinking, "Okay, which one should I use?" There isn't a general rule for this. Arrays and List<T> can serve the same purpose. You can find a lot of additional information online to convince you to use one or the other.

Arrays are generally faster. For what we are doing at this stage, we don't need to worry about processing speeds. Some time from now, however, you might need a bit more speed if your game slows down, so this is good to remember.

List<T> offers great flexibility. You don't need to know the size of the list during declaration. There is a massive list of *out-of-the-box* operations that you can use with List, so it is my recommendation. Array is faster, List<T> is more flexible.

Retrieving the data from the Array or List<T>

Declaring and storing data in the array or list is very clear to us now. The next thing to learn is how to get stored elements from an array. To get a stored element from the array, write an array variable name followed by square brackets. You must write an int value within the brackets. That value is called an index. The index is simply a position in the array. So, to get the first element stored in the array, we will write the following code:

```
myArray[0];
```

Unity will return the data stored in the first place in myArray. It works exactly the same way as the return type methods that we discussed in the previous chapter. So, if myArray stores a string value on index 0, that string will be returned to the place where you are calling it. Complex? It's not. Let's show you by example.

 The index value starts at 0, no 1, so the first element in an array containing 10 elements will be accessible through an index value of 0 and last one through a value of 9.

Let's extend the familyMembers example:

```
1  using UnityEngine;
2  using System.Collections;
3  using System.Collections.Generic;
4
5
6  public class LearningLists : MonoBehaviour {
7
8
9      public List<string> familyMembers = new List<string>();
10
11
12     void Start() {
13
14         familyMembers.Add("Greg");
15         familyMembers.Add("Kate");
16         familyMembers.Add("Adam");
17         familyMembers.Add("Mia");
18
19
20         string thirdFamilyMember = familyMembers[2];
21         Debug.Log(thirdFamilyMember);
22
23     }
24
25  }
26
27
```

I want to talk about line **20**. The rest of it is pretty obvious for you, isn't it? Line **20** creates a new variable called `thirdFamilyMember` and assigns the third value stored in the `familyMembers` list. We are using an index value of 2 instead of 3 because in programming counting starts at 0. Try to memorize this; it is a common mistake made by beginners in programming.

Go ahead and click **Play**. You will see the name **Adam** being printed in the Unity **Console**. While accessing objects stored in an array, make sure you use an index value between zero and the size of the array. In simpler words, we cannot access data from index 10 in an array that contains only four objects. Makes sense?

Checking the size

This is very common; we need to check the size of the array or list. There is a slight difference between a C# array and `List<T>`.

To get the size as an integer value, we write the name of the variable, then a dot, and then `Length` of an array or `Count` for `List<T>`:

- `arrayName.Length`: This returns an integer value with the size of the array
- `listName.Count`: This returns an integer value with the size of the list

As we need to focus on one of the choices here and move on, from now on we will be using `List<T>`.

ArrayList

We definitely know how to use lists now. We also know how to declare a new list and add, remove, and retrieve elements. Moreover, you have learned that the data stored in `List<T>` must be of the same type across all elements. Let's throw a little curveball.

`ArrayList` is basically `List<T>` without a specified type of data. This means that we can store whatever objects we want. Storing elements of different types is also possible. `ArrayList` is very flexible.

Take a look at the following example to understand what `ArrayList` can look like:

```
1  using UnityEngine;
2  using System.Collections;
3
4  public class LearningArrayList : MonoBehaviour {
5
6
7      public ArrayList inventory = new ArrayList();
8
9
10     void Start() {
11
12         inventory.Add(10);
13         inventory.Add(20);
14         inventory.Add("Adam");
15         inventory.Add(GameObject.Find("Player"));
16
17
18         Debug.Log(inventory[1].GetType());
19         Debug.Log(inventory[2].GetType());
20
21     }
22
23
24  }
```

You have probably noticed that `ArrayList` also supports all common operations, such as `.Add()`. Lines **12** to **15** add different elements into the array. The first two are of the `integer` type, the third is a `string` type, and the last one is a `GameObject`. All mixed types of elements in one variable!

When using `ArrayList`, you might need to check what type of element is under a specific index to know how to treat it in code. Unity provides a very useful function that you can use on virtually any type of object. Its `GetType()` method returns the type of the object, not the value. We are using it in lines **18** and **19** to print the types of the second and third elements.

Go ahead, write the preceding code, and click **Play**. You should get the following output in the **Console** window:

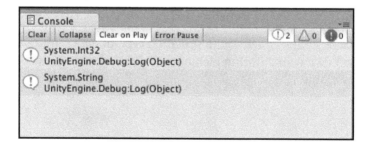

Dictionaries

When we talk about collection data, we need to mention Dictionaries. A Dictionary is similar to a List. However, instead of accessing a certain element by index value, we use a string called key.

The Dictionary that you will probably be using the most often is called Hashtable. Feel free to dive into the C# documentation after reading this chapter to discover all the bits of this powerful class.

Here are a few key properties of Hashtable:

- Hashtable can be resized dynamically, like List<T> and ArrayList
- Hashtable can store multiple data types at the same type, like ArrayList
- A public member Hashtable isn't visible in the Unity **Inspector** panel due to default inspector limitations

I want to make sure that you won't feel confused, so I will go straight to a simple example:

```csharp
using UnityEngine;
using System.Collections;

public class LearningDictionaries : MonoBehaviour {

    public Hashtable personalDetails = new Hashtable();


    void Start() {

        personalDetails.Add("firstName", "Greg");
        personalDetails.Add("lastName", "Lukosek");
        personalDetails.Add("gender", "male");
        personalDetails.Add("isMarried", true);
        personalDetails.Add("age", 29);

    }

}
```

Accessing values

To access a specific key in the `Hashtable`, you must know the string key the value is stored under. Remember, the key is the first value in the brackets when adding an element to `Hashtable`. Ideally, you should also know the type of data you are trying to access. In most cases, that would not be an issue. Take a look at this line:

```
Debug.Log((string)personalDetails["firstName"]);
```

We already know that using `Debug.Log` serves to display a message on the Unity console, so what are we trying to display? A `string` value (it's one that can contain letters and numbers), then we specify where that value is stored. In this case, the information is stored under `Hashtable personalDetails` and the content that we want to display is `firstName`.

Now take a look at the script once again and see if you can display the age, remember that the value that we are trying to access here is a number, so we should use `int` instead of `string`:

```
1  using UnityEngine;
2  using System.Collections;
3
4  public class LearningDictionaries : MonoBehaviour {
5
6      public Hashtable personalDetails = new Hashtable();
7
8
9      void Start() {
10
11         personalDetails.Add("firstName", "Greg");
12         personalDetails.Add("lastName", "Lukosek");
13         personalDetails.Add("gender", "male");
14         personalDetails.Add("isMarried", true);
15         personalDetails.Add("age", 29);
16
17     }
18
19  }
20
21
```

Similar to `ArrayList`, we can store mixed-type data in `Hashtable`. Unity requires the developer to specify how an accessed element should be treated. To do this, we need to cast the element into a specific data type. The syntax is very simple. There are brackets with the data type inside, followed by the `Hashtable` variable name. Then, in square brackets, we have to enter the key string the value is stored under. Ufff, confusing!

As you can see in the preceding line, we are casting to string (inside brackets). If we were to access another type of data, for example, an integer number, the syntax would look like this:

```
(int)personalDetails["age"];
```

I hope that this is clear now. If it isn't, why not search for more examples on the Unity forums?

How do I know what's inside my Hashtable?

Hashtable, by default, isn't displayed in the Unity **Inspector** panel. You cannot simply look at the **Inspector** tab and preview all keys and values in your public member Hashtable.

We can do this in code, however. You know how to access a value and cast it. What if you are trying to access the value under a key that isn't stored in the Hashtable? Unity will spit out a null reference error and your program is likely to crash.

To check whether an element exists in the Hashtable, we can use the .Contains(object) method, passing the key parameter:

```
18
19      if (personalDetails.Contains("firstName")) {
20          Debug.Log((string)personalDetails["firstName"]);
21      }
22      else {
23          Debug.Log("First name isnt stored in the hashtable");
24      }
25
```

This determines whether the array contains the item and if so, the code will continue; otherwise, it will stop there, preventing any error.

Summary

In this chapter, you learned how to use collections of data. You now know what an array is, what List<T> is, and how to use Hashtable. If you haven't fully understood this chapter, I suggest a quick read through it again. In the next chapter, we will move on to something more advanced: loops.

6

Loops

In previous chapters, we learned how to tell Unity what to do line by line. In most of our examples, we wrote one instruction per line. I want to move on to something a bit more complex now.

In this chapter, we will cover the following topics:

- Introduction to loops
- Why we use loops
- Commonly used loops
- Loops with statements
- Searching for data inside a loop
- Breaking loop execution

Introduction to loops

Loops are an essential technique when writing any software in pretty much any programming language. By using loops, we gain the ability to repeat a block of code x number of times. There are many variants of loops in C#. We will talk about the most common loops:

- The `foreach` loop
- The `for` loop
- The `while` loop

The foreach loop

The foreach loop is very simple to use. It also has the simplest syntax. We use the foreach keyword followed by brackets in this loop. Inside the brackets, you must specify the type of data you want to iterate through inside your loop. Pick a single element variable name. You can name it whatever you like. This name is used to access this variable inside the main loop block. After the name, we write the in keyword, followed by our List variable name, as shown here:

```
foreach (Type elementName in myCollectionVariable) {
    //loop block
}
```

I know it's quite confusing now, but don't worry too much about the theory. All you need to know as of now is that the code inside the foreach loop is called as many times as there are elements in myCollectionVariable. So, if myCollectionVariable contains 10 elements, the code inside the loop block (highlighted in pink) will be executed 10 times.

To make it a bit more *eye friendly*, let's look at an actual code example. We will use the family members example from the previous chapter and print every element inside the loop on the Unity **Console**:

```
1  using UnityEngine;
2  using System.Collections;
3  using System.Collections.Generic;
4
5  public class LearningLoopsForeach : MonoBehaviour {
6
7
8      public List<string> familyMembers = new List<string>();
9
10
11     void Start() {
12
13         familyMembers.Add("Greg");
14         familyMembers.Add("Kate");
15         familyMembers.Add("Adam");
16         familyMembers.Add("Mia");
17
18
19
20         foreach (string familyMember in familyMembers) {
21
22             Debug.Log(familyMember);
23
24         }
25
26     }
27
28 }
```

Write the preceding code, add it as a component to a GameObject, and click **Play**. Line **20** creates the loop (foreach familyMember in familyMembers).

Lines **21** to **23** form a loop block. As our List contains four elements, this code block will be executed four times, each time with a different value stored in the familyMember local variable.

Line **22** simply prints the output on the Unity **Console**. Your output should look like this:

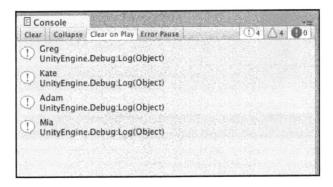

Not that scary, isn't it? Go ahead and play around with the code. You can, for example, add more elements to the `familyMembers` List.

Alternatively, you can print the number of characters each element has and so on. The sky is the limit! The `foreach` loop can be used with any type of collection, so there are no issues with using it with an `Array`, `ArrayList`, or even `Hashtable`.

The for loop

You have learned about `foreach` loops. When iterating through a `foreach` loop, we can use a local variable directly to access the data we need. In a `for` loop, we also create a variable. However, it is an integer variable for controlling the execution of the loop and accessing the data inside the collection by index.

There are three fundamental parts of the `for` loop. It will look a bit scary to you at the beginning, but try not to run away:

```
for( int i = 0; i < 10; i++) {

    //loop block

}
```

The `for` loop's syntax might look overcomplicated, but trust me, it isn't! Let's go through its elements one by one.

The `for` loop begins with the `for` keyword, followed by brackets. Inside the brackets we must have three fundamental elements separated by semicolons:

- **Initializer**: The initializer is simply a declared variable that is assigned a value. In the preceding code, we declared a variable called `i` of the `int` type and assigned it a value of `0`.
- **Condition**: The condition must be true for the code block to be executed. In this example, the loop will run through the code block only if the `i` variable is less than `10`.
- **Iterator**: The iterator, `i++` in this case, simply adds a value of `1` to the mentioned variable every time the loop completes an execution.

In simple words, to use a `for` loop, we need an integer variable to control it. The initializer is the declaration and assignment of that variable. In most cases, you will never have to change it and it will always look like this:

```
int i = 0;
```

The next step is to describe under what conditions the loop will be running. It is the same type of condition that you might write in any `if` statement. If i is less than 10, this statement is true. If this statement is true, our loop will execute whatever code is inside the code block:

```
i < 10;
```

The last part of the `for` loop's syntax is simply the addition of 1 to the previous value stored in the i variable. The i++ might look rather scary, but it's simply a more elegant version of this statement: `i = i+1;`.

> The ++ operator increments the value by 1.

I have introduced a lot of technical words here. Try not to panic. Remember that we want to take baby steps, as we need to make sure you fully understand `for` loops. I will show it in an example. Let's now write some proper code using a `for` loop.

An example

Let's create a new C# script and call it `learningLoopsFor`:

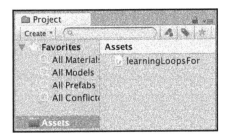

Then we open the script and we are going to create a `List` that will contain the names of the family members. We always start the script by writing down the variables that we'll be using, in this case it will be the `List<string>`:

```
public class learningLoopsFor : MonoBehaviour {

    public List<string> familyMembers = new List <string> ();
```

After that, we need to add the family members to our `List` and we are going to do all that inside the `void Start()`:

```
1 using System.Collections;
2 using System.Collections.Generic;
3 using UnityEngine;
4 using NUnit.Framework;
5
6 public class learningLoopsFor : MonoBehaviour {
7
8
9     public List<string> familyMembers = new List <string> ();
10
11
12     void Start () {
13
14         familyMembers.Add ("Greg");
15         familyMembers.Add ("Kate");
16         familyMembers.Add ("Adam");
17         familyMembers.Add ("Mia");
18
19         }
20     }
21
22 }
23
```

To conclude our script now, we are going to write the `for loop` and this is the most important part, so if you don't understand it right away, don't worry, it will be explained in detail what we are doing:

```
1 using System.Collections;
2 using System.Collections.Generic;
3 using UnityEngine;
4 using NUnit.Framework;
5
6 public class learningLoopsFor : MonoBehaviour {
7
8
9     public List<string> familyMembers = new List <string> ();
10
11
12     void Start () {
13
14         familyMembers.Add ("Greg");
15         familyMembers.Add ("Kate");
16         familyMembers.Add ("Adam");
17         familyMembers.Add ("Mia");
18
19
20         for (int i = 0; i < familyMembers.Count; i++) {
21
22             //loop block
23             Debug.Log(familyMembers[i]);
24         }
25     }
26
27 }
28
```

What we are trying to do in this example is iterate through all the elements inside the familyMembers list and print their values to the Unity Console; we can test this by assigning the script to any object of the game (we have chosen the camera) and click **Play**:

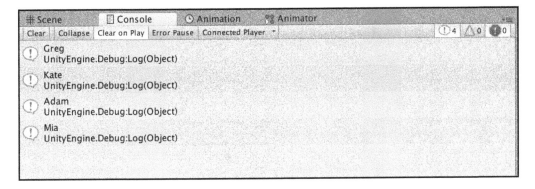

You will probably ask, "Why do I even have to learn this? I could have used a foreach loop." Correct! A foreach loop is definitely a good approach to this task. However, there will be cases when you need to know at what index position in the array a certain element is stored. That is when you will use a for loop instead of a foreach. Trust me, it's worth it!

Line **20** constructs our `for` loop. As I promised before, in most cases there is no need to edit the initializer at all.

Take a look at this condition:

```
i < familyMembers.Count;
```

Previously, we used a value of `10` directly in the condition. In the current example, we want to iterate through all the elements in the array. We don't always know the size of our array, so the safest option is to access its size directly. If you are still confused, please go back `Chapter 5`, *Lists, Arrays, and Dictionaries*, where we spoke about checking out the size of an array and `List<T>`.

Let's observe what actually happens when you click the **Play** button.

Unity executes the `Start()` function. Lines **14** to **17** add four string values to the `familyMembers` list.

Unity starts executing the loop from line **20**. It creates the `i` variable with a value of `0`. Then it checks the condition. As `0` is smaller than the size of the list, the code block is executed with a value of `0` for `i`.

Line **23** accesses the value in the first place in the `familyMembers` list as the value of `i` is `0`. Unity prints the `"Greg"` string.

Unity hits the end of the loop block and goes back to line **20** to check whether the loop should run through again.

But first, `i++` increments the value of `i` by `1`. So `0 + 1 = 1`. The `i` variable is now equal to `1`. Unity checks the condition again and runs through the loop block again.

These steps will keep occurring until the `i < familyMembers.Count;` condition becomes `false`. This condition will be `false` simply when `i` becomes equal to `4`. Then, Unity won't execute the code block anymore but will proceed with the normal execution order outside the loop.

The while loop

There is one more type of loop that I want to talk about. It has pretty much the simplest form of any loop. The `while` loop does not create any variable to control its execution. To create a `while` loop, start with the keyword `while`, followed by brackets. Within the brackets, you must write a condition. Whenever the condition is true, the code inside the loop block will be executed:

```
while (condition) {

    //loop block

}
```

It's worth knowing that this is quite a dangerous loop and you need to know how to use it. As a `while` loop does not create a control variable and is not iterating through the `List`, there is a possible scenario where a condition is always true. This will create an infinite loop-a loop that will go on forever. An infinite loop never finishes executing the loop block, and most certainly it will crash your program and even the Unity **Editor**.

To avoid this nasty situation - when Unity crashes and we don't even know why we can use a variable to control the flow of the `while` loop like we did in our `for` loop. Then, this is what the loop looks like:

```
19
20          int i = 0;
21
22          while (i<10) {
23
24              //loop block
25              Debug.Log(i);
26              i++;
27          }
28
29
```

You have seen this before, right? This example contains exactly the same fundamental elements as a `for` loop. Line **20** is an initializer, and within line **22**, we have the `i<10` conditions. The iterator is on line **26**.

Go ahead and type in the code. Try to predict what will happen in the **Console** window before you press **Play** in editor.

while versus for loops

Both the `while` and `for` loops do the same thing. I bet you are wondering why we should even bother learning them both. A `for` loop is great for iterations through arrays and lists. A `while` loop is great for holding code execution until a condition isn't met.

I don't want you to worry about `while` loops for now. We will go through more complex examples when you learn about coroutines in Unity. A coroutine is a special type of method in Unity that can run through an infinite loop without crashing. Let's forget it for a few chapters. We will definitely use them in the second half of the book when you build your first game!

Loops in statements

You have learned the fundamentals of the three basic loops. Let's have some fun now. You can write virtually any code inside a loop block.

Why don't we insert some `if` statements inside our code block and ask Unity to make the decisions? Let's iterate through a `for` loop 100 times and print on the Unity **Console** some useful information about the `i` variable's value, as follows:

```
1    using UnityEngine;
2    using System.Collections;
3
4    public class LearningLoopsWithStatements : MonoBehaviour {
5
6
7        void Start () {
8
9            for( int i = 0; i < 100; i++) {
10
11               if (i == 0) {
12                   Debug.Log(i + " is zero");
13               }
14               else if (IsNumberEven(i)) {
15                   Debug.Log(i + " is even");
16               }
17               else {
18                   Debug.Log(i + " is odd");
19               }
20            }
21        }
22
23
24        public bool IsNumberEven(int number) {
25
26            if (number % 2 == 0) {
27                return true;
28            }
29            else {
30                return false;
31            }
32        }
33
34
35    }
36
37
38
```

Checking whether a number is zero, even, or odd

Let's analyze the code:

- **Line 9**: This is the declaration of the `for` loop. The condition of our loop is `i < 100`, which means that we will run the loop 100 times with the value of `i` increasing from 0 to 99.
- **Line 11**: This contains a simple `if` statement that checks whether `i` is equal to `0`. As the `i` value increments every time the loop runs through, line **12** will be executed only once, on the first loop run.
- **Line 14**: This contains `if` statements that call the `IsNumberEven` function, which returns `bool`. I know this feels very complicated now, but it is deliberate. We need to make sure that you understand every single line of this example.

To make things easier, we can talk about the `IsNumberEven` method first.

The IsNumberEven method is constructed from elements that are well known to you. This method takes one int parameter and uses name number within itself. It also returns bool. That's why we can use it directly in line **14**.

Modulo

Take a look at line **26**. The % operator is called **modulo**. Modulo computes a remainder. The modulo operator provides a way to execute code once in every several iterations of a loop. We are using modulo here to check whether a number variable can be perfectly divided by 2. If the number can be divided, the remainder will be equal to 0, so we will have an even number! Otherwise, the number must be odd.

Coming back to line **14**, a method is a substitute for a value and IsEvenMethod is a return type method, returning Boolean value inside if statement. In simpler words, when the value of i is passed to IsEvenNumber, the method returns a true or false value. If the value is true, line **15** will be executed and the message will be printed on the **Console** window.

Let's test the code. If all goes well, you should see lots of messages printed on the **Console** window, as follows:

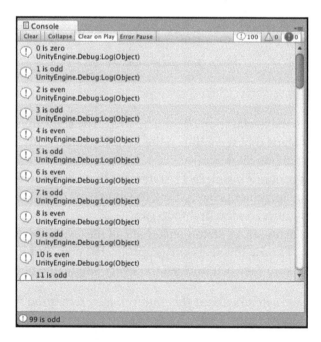

All went very well then! Go ahead and try to experiment with this code. Why not run the loop 1,000 times? Do it! Computers can perform mathematical calculations at amazing speeds.

Searching for data inside an array

Very often, you will need to get a single element inside an array. It's very straightforward, as long as you know the specific index your element is stored under. If you don't, you can search for it by iterating through the entire array object.

Yet again, let's go back to the `familyMembers` example and try to look for the index of the "Adam" string value:

```
using UnityEngine;
using System.Collections;
using System.Collections.Generic;

public class LearningLoopsSearching : MonoBehaviour {

    public List<string> familyMembers = new List<string>();

    void Start() {

        familyMembers.Add("Greg");
        familyMembers.Add("Kate");
        familyMembers.Add("Adam");
        familyMembers.Add("Mia");


        int adamsIndex = -1;

        for( int i = 0; i < familyMembers.Count; i++) {

            if (familyMembers[i] == "Adam") {
                adamsIndex = i;
                break;
            }
        }


        if (adamsIndex == -1) {
            Debug.Log("Adam value is not stored in the list");
        }
        else {
            Debug.Log("Adam value found at index " + adamsIndex);
        }

    }
}
```

We are not going too much into the details. The easiest way of finding the index of a certain element in the collection is by looping through the array and comparing elements. You can spot that on line **22**. If the `familyMembers[i] == "Adam"` condition is true, line **23** will be executed. The `adamsIndex` variable will then be assigned the current `i` value.

Notice the default value of `adamsIndex`. I deliberately assigned it −1 so that we can check on line **29** whether there were any changes to this value inside the loop. If it's still −1, it means that the value we are trying to find inside the array was not found at all.

Breaking the loop

Loops can also be designed to stop themselves from executing any further. To do this, we use the `break` keyword. Whenever Unity executes a line containing the `break` keyword, it will stop the loop it is in and continue executing from the line just after the loop block.

We use `break` mainly for performance reasons. In the preceding example, we are looking for the `"Adam"` string. Once we've found it, there is no reason to iterate through the remaining elements of the loop. So, line **24** breaks the loop and the execution jumps to just after the loop block, line **27**.

Summary

Hey! You are doing really well. In this chapter, you learned how to *ask* Unity to loop through sections of code and do something useful. In Chapter 7, *Object, a Container with Variables and Methods*, we will dive into the subject of organizing your code and object-oriented programming.

7
Object, a Container with Variables and Methods

We have covered most of the theory part now. You can read and write code. In this chapter, we will discuss organizing your code and object-oriented programming.

In this chapter, we will cover the following topics:

- Working with objects
- Constructing the class and its syntax
- Using C# constructors with data

Working with objects is a class act

Throughout the book, we have been talking about objects without worrying too much about what exactly means or what it is. It can be confusing at first because we know what an object is in real life, it's practically everything that humankind has created, a phone, a computer, pen, paper, keyboard, keys, all these are objects, but can we say the same regarding Unity objects? To simplify the answer, everything that we put inside of our scene inside Unity, is an object.

It doesn't matter if it's the playable character or a background image; everything that we create or add inside the scene automatically becomes an object. In the virtual world of gaming, most people consider things they can see on the screen to be objects:

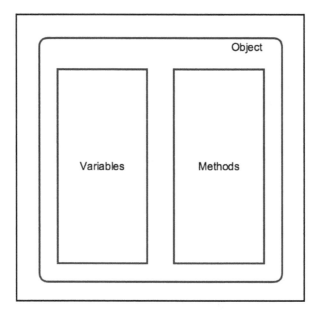

If you can expand your mind just a little bit more, perhaps you can accept that not all objects in Unity have to be something you can see in a game **Scene**. In fact, the vast majority of objects in Unity are not visible in the **Scene**.

In a computer, an object is just a small section of your computer's memory that acts like a container. The container can have some data stored in variables and some methods to work with the data.

The best example I can show you is the object you've been using since we started this book:

```
1 ⊟ using UnityEngine;
2 └ using System.Collections;
3
4 ⊟ public class LearningScript : MonoBehaviour {
5  |
6  |      // Use this for initialization
7 ⊟     void Start () {
8  |
9  ├      }
10 |
11 |      // Update is called once per frame
12 ⊟     void Update () {
13 |
14 ├      }
15 └ }
16
```

In MonoDevelop, we've been working with script called `LearningScript`. In Unity, we use the general term script, but it's actually a class, which means it's a definition of a type of container. Look at line 4 of the file:

```
public class LearningScript : MonoBehaviour
```

See that second word? It means that `LearningScript` is a class. In this class, we defined its member variables and methods. Any variable not declared in a method is a member variable of the class.

In `Chapter 2`, *Introducing the Building Blocks for Unity Scripts*, I told you about the magic that happens when we attach the `script` class to a `GameObject`. The script becomes a Component.

Besides the visual mesh in the **Scene**, can you visualize in your mind that a `GameObject` is just a bunch of different types of Component objects assembled together to construct that `GameObject`? Each of those individual Components shown in the **Inspector** window will become an object in our computer's memory when we click the **Play** button.

Select any `GameObject` in the **Scene** window and look at the **Inspector**. For example, select the **Main Camera** `GameObject`. There are several Components on the **Main Camera** `GameObject`.

Look at each of these defined Components. Every one of these Components started off as a `class` file in Unity, defining a type of container for variables and methods:

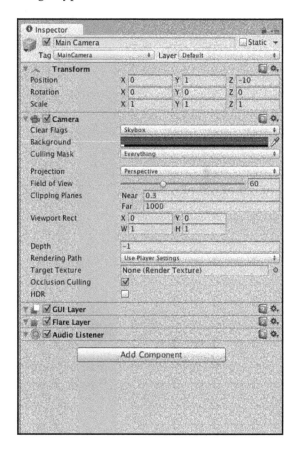

A few facts

We don't see or modify those Unity `class` files, but they're in Unity somewhere:

- The name of the class is also known as the object type of the object that will be created in memory from that class when the **Play** button is clicked.
- Just like `int` or a string is a type of data, the name of a class is also a type of data.

- When we declare a variable and specify the type of data it will store, it can easily just store a reference to an object of the `LearningScript` type, as shown in the following line of code:

```
LearningScript myVariable;
```

- Storing a reference to an object in a variable does not mean we are storing the actual object. It means we are storing the location in the memory of that object. It's just a reference that points to the object in memory so that the computer knows where to access the object's data and methods. This means we can have several variables storing a reference to the same object, but there's still only one actual object in memory.

A script is just a file on your hard drive, and there's only ever one file. The `class` file simply defines a type of container of variables and methods that will become a Component object in the memory when you click **Play**. You can attach the script to many `GameObjects`, but there's still only one file on your hard drive.

Attaching a script to a `GameObject` is like placing a sticky note on the `GameObject`. When we click the **Play** button, Unity looks at our `GameObject` and sees the sticky note that says "This `GameObject` is supposed to have a Component of type `LearningScript`. Make some room in the computer's memory to hold this object of variables and methods, as described in the `LearningScript` class file."

If we were to attach `LearningScript` to 1,000 `GameObjects` and click **Play**, there will be 1,000 separate sections created in your computer's memory, with each storing an object of the `LearningScript` type. Each one has its own set of variables and methods, as described by the `script` file. Each one of those 1,000 sections of computer memory is a separate Component object of its respective `GameObject`.

Even though the object created from a class is called a `Component` by Unity, in general in C#, each object that gets created from a class is called an instance object.

Your brain is probably just about to start boiling. To make this easier to understand, let's write a quick example.

Example

For this example, we are going to create a new script called `Person` and the first thing that we need to do is to remove the default `MonoBehaviour` from our code:

```
1 using System.Collections;
2 using System.Collections.Generic;
3 using UnityEngine;
4
5 public class Person : MonoBehaviour {
6
7     // Use this for initialization
8     void Start () {
9
10     }
11
12     // Update is called once per frame
13     void Update () {
14
15     }
16 }
17
```

By removing the `MonoBehaviour` part, we are saying that this script is a class named `Person`. The main reason is that we treat the `Person` class as a simple container of the data, a C# object of type `Person`, not a Unity Component. We don't need this class to be a full–spec Unity Component.

Then we can add any type of information that we want: string, int, bool, and so on. For this example, we have written some basic information that we can ask about a person:

```
1 using System.Collections;
2 using System.Collections.Generic;
3 using UnityEngine;
4
5 public class Person : MonoBehaviour {
6
7     public string firstName = "";
8     public string lastName = "";
9     public int age = 0;
10    public string address = "";
11    public bool isMale = false;
12    public bool isMarried = false;
13 }
14
```

As you can see, you can easily store any type of data inside your class. We make variables public as we will need to access this data from other classes.

Instantiating an object

We know exactly how to write a class as an object. The next step would be creating an instance of the object of that class. In C#, we use the `new` keyword to instantiate the object.

The syntax looks like this:

```
new ObjectType();
```

So, we are using the `new` keyword followed by an `ObjectType`, and then we have the opening and closing brackets. `ObjectType` is just your class name (we discussed this before).

Each time you instantiate an object of any class, Unity will create some space in the memory to store that object. The issue in the preceding syntax is that we are not assigning that freshly created object anywhere. Therefore, we won't be able to access its data.

The best way is to assign this object to a variable:

```
ObjectType myObjectInstance = new ObjectType();
```

This way, we can access and change any variables inside our `myObjectInstance` object using the dot syntax. Again, let's learn from examples; OOP might seem a bit confusing at the start, but I promise you will master it by the time you've finished the whole book:

```
1  using UnityEngine;
2  using System.Collections;
3
4  public class Family : MonoBehaviour {
5
6
7      public Person father;
8      public Person mother;
9      public Person son;
10
11
12     void Start() {
13
14         father = new Person();
15         father.firstName = "Greg";
16         father.lastName = "Lukosek";
17         father.age = 29;
18         father.isMale = true;
19         father.isMarried = true;
20
21
22         mother = new Person();
23         mother.firstName = "Kate";
24         mother.lastName = "Lukosek";
25         mother.age = 28;
26         mother.isMale = false;
27         mother.isMarried = true;
28
29
30         son = new Person();
31         son.firstName = "Adam";
32         son.lastName = "Lukosek";
33         son.age = 3;
34         son.isMale = true;
35         son.isMarried = false;
36
37
38
39         Debug.Log(father.firstName + " and " + mother.firstName +
40             " have a beautiful son " + son.firstName);
41
42
43     }
44  }
45
46
```

Please write the preceding code. We are using the `Person` class we spoke about a bit earlier; make sure you have the `Person` class in your project too. In lines **7** to **9**, we are declaring a public member variable of type `Person`.

In line **14**, we are instantiating a new object of type `Person` and assigning it to a public member named `father`. In lines **15** to **19**, we are assigning various bits of data to the `father` variable. Please notice the syntax. To access the variables inside our object, we write the name of the instance variable followed by the dot and the name of the public variable. You can only access public variables and methods this way. Private variables are not accessible from other classes. In the same way, we have instantiated and assigned `mother` and `son` objects.

In line **39**, we are printing a quick message composed from the data stored inside the `father`, `mother`, and `son` objects. Press **Play** in Unity and your **Console** output should look like this:

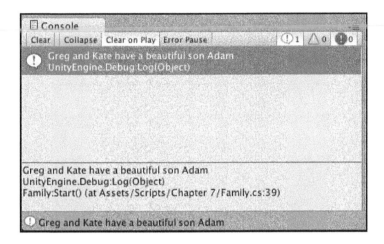

Go ahead and experiment with the code, change it, and play with it!

Bored yet?

I understand that you might feel a bit frustrated now. We are learning a lot about theory, going through examples, and it isn't exciting at all. I promised fun and we will get there, but I must make sure that you understand the fundamentals of OOP. This knowledge will help us design a cool–looking game that is coded using clean practices. Code can be good and bad, and it can be written in a way that is easily understood by other developers or it might be unmanageable and messy.

By learning how to organize your code, you absorb and use good practices that will help you to be a top developer who is proud of their code. So stay focused! Let's go through the theory and make an awesome game later.

> *"Any fool can write code that a computer can understand. Good programmers write code that humans can understand."*

- *Martin Fowler*

Using methods with objects

We learned that an object is a container for data. We can store specific data inside the object in its variables, and we can also write some more useful methods. OOP is a very neat and flexible concept. There is nothing stopping us from using our encapsulated object and passing it as a parameter to the other method. Let's write the following code as an example, where the class name is `Person`:

```
using UnityEngine;
using System.Collections;

public class Person {

    public string firstName = "";
    public string lastName = "";
    public Person spouse;


    public Person () {

    }


    public Person (string pFirstName, string pLastName) {
        this.firstName = pFirstName;
        this.lastName = pLastName;
    }


    public bool IsMarriedWith (Person otherPerson) {

        if (spouse != null) {
            //Person object is stored in spouse variable
            if (otherPerson == this.spouse) {
                //otherPerson object is the same as stored spouse
                return true;
            }
            else {
                //not married
                return false;
            }
        }
        else {
            //spouse variable is not assigned so this
            //Person is not married at all
            return false;
        }
    }
}
```

I removed most of the variables from the `Person` class to make this example clearer. If you are writing this example in the same Unity Project as the previous example, you will get some errors in the `Family` class we were using before. I recommend starting this example, in a new Unity Project and the class here is `LearningObjects`:

```
1  using UnityEngine;
2  using System.Collections;
3
4  public class LearningObjects : MonoBehaviour {
5
6
7      public Person man;
8      public Person woman;
9
10
11
12     void Start() {
13
14         man = new Person();
15         man.firstName = "Greg";
16         man.lastName = "Lukosek";
17
18         woman = new Person();
19         woman.firstName = "Kate";
20         woman.lastName = "Lukosek";
21
22         man.spouse = woman;
23         woman.spouse = man;
24
25
26         if (man.IsMarriedWith(woman)) {
27             Debug.Log(man.firstName + " is married to " + woman.firstName);
28         }
29         else {
30             Debug.Log(man.firstName + " and " + woman.firstName + " are not married");
31         }
32     }
33
34 }
35
36
```

Yes, lots of new code to analyze, awesome! What we are trying to do here is create two instances of the Person object. We'll cross–reference them by assigning a public member spouse, and then call the method within the object class itself. Let's analyze this step by step, as we do not want to get you confused.

Let's talk about the Person class first. You most certainly understand what an object is and that we can hold variables in them. However, I want to talk about the IsMarriedWith method inside the class itself. As you can see, this is a return type method that returns a bool value and takes one parameter. Notice the type of the parameter. The IsMarriedWith method takes another instance of the Person class.

Line **13** of the Person class checks whether there is any value stored in the spouse variable.

The easiest way to check whether there is any value assigned to the variable is by comparing the variable to null. If the variable isn't null, it means there is something assigned to the variable.

The null keyword is a literal that represents a null reference, one that does not refer to any object. It is the default value of reference–type variables.

So, if spouse isn't assigned, it means our instance isn't married and we are returning `false` in line **27**. Let's talk about the `LearningObjects` class. It must be pretty obvious to you what is going on there. We are creating two instances of the `Person` class and assigning the values. Notice lines **22** and **23**. We are assigning `woman.spouse` to a `man` object and `man.spouse` to a `woman` object. I asked you to do it this way to demonstrate that you can easily reference objects, inside other objects even if both of them are the same type.

Line **26** is where the main logic happens. We are calling the `IsMarriedWith` method on the `man` instance and passing the `woman` object. Yet again, this is to demonstrate how flexible objects are. The condition in line **26** will be true if two `Person` type objects are married. If so, a suitable message is printed out in the Unity **Console** panel.

Go ahead and play with the code. Try to add some more methods or variables to the `Person` class. Why not add an `age` public member again and write a method to return the total number of years? The sky is the limit! The best you can do is write a lot of code. Learning by experience is the fastest way to become a decent programmer. Fingers crossed!

Custom constructors

We saw how to create a new instance of an object using the following syntax:

```
new ObjectType();
```

This way, you are calling the public implicit constructor. In simple words, the default constructor creates an instance without taking any parameters. All C# objects that are not using custom constructors will be using an implicit constructor.

Another great tactic is to write your own constructors. Why? It will have you typing a lot of code, it's fun to do, and it makes code much easier to read.

Custom constructors should be written within the code block of the class. Have a look at the example first and then we'll go through the actual syntax. A custom public constructor for the `Person` class could look like this:

```
public Person (string pFirstName, string pLastName) {
    this.firstName = pFirstName;
    this.lastName = pLastName;
}
```

As you can see, it's nothing scary. A custom constructor is a public method that takes some parameters. The generic syntax for the public constructor will always start with the `public` keyword followed by a class name. Inside the brackets, we can write any parameters we want.

I try to keep my code consistent and I have a simple naming rule for constructor parameters. I always use a lowercase *p* followed by the parameter name. This way, I avoid confusion inside the constructor body. So, the `firstName` parameter is called `pFirstName` and the `lastName` parameter is called `pLastName`. Feel free to set your own rule for this. However, this one is quite common. I saw it being used by another developer and adopted it.

Let's try to implement it now. Add the two constructors to the `Person` method:

```
1  using UnityEngine;
2  using System.Collections;
3
4  public class Person {
5
6      public string firstName = "";
7      public string lastName = "";
8      public Person spouse;
9
10
11     public Person () {
12
13     }
14
15
16     public Person (string pFirstName, string pLastName) {
17         this.firstName = pFirstName;
18         this.lastName = pLastName;
19     }
20
21
22     public bool IsMarriedWith (Person otherPerson) {
23
24         if (spouse != null) {
25             //Person object is stored in spouse variable
26             if (otherPerson == this.spouse) {
27                 //otherPerson object is the same as stored spouse
28                 return true;
29             }
30             else {
31                 //not married
32                 return false;
33             }
34         }
35         else {
36             //spouse variable is not assigned so this
37             //Person is not married at all
38             return false;
39         }
40     }
41
42 }
43
```

You are probably wondering why we are adding an empty constructor at all. It's simply to keep a bit of flexibility if we want to instantiate the object without any data. This way, we will also stop any errors coming up inside the `LearningObjects` class, as we are using an implicit constructor there.

Let's focus on the constructor within lines **16** to **19**. As you can see, there's nothing scary. It is exactly what you would expect to see, right? We are taking two string parameters, naming them according to the *p* rule, and assigning them to the variables within this object.

Overloading

To understand how to use custom constructors, we need to learn a bit about different overloads. Overloading happens when we have two methods with the same name but different signatures, that is, we are passing different types of parameters into the method.

As a constructor is a public method, the same rule applies. You can choose what overload you want to use simply by entering the specific parameters when calling the method. MonoDevelop works well with Unity and helps you preview the available overloads you can use with its parameters and type.

Go back to `LearningObjects` and have a try. Inside the `Start` function, type `new Person ()`. The popup in MonoDevelop will appear as soon as you type the open bracket:

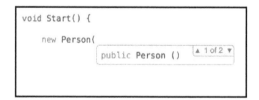

MonoDevelop is trying to let us know there are two overloads available for `Person` constructors. Press down the arrow on your keyboard straight away to preview the next overload:

```
void Start() {

    new Person(
                          public Person (          ▲ 2 of 2 ▼
                            string pFirstName,
                            string pLastName
                          )
}
```

As you can see, this is the custom constructor we have written. By pressing the arrow key whenever you see this popup, you can iterate through all available overloads.

We know how to write custom public constructors and how to call them. Let's try to put that knowledge to use now. I will use the same example again to make it easier to compare:

```
1  using UnityEngine;
2  using System.Collections;
3
4  public class LearningObjectsWithConstructors : MonoBehaviour {
5
6
7      public Person man;
8      public Person woman;
9
10
11
12      void Start() {
13
14          man = new Person("Greg", "Lukosek");
15          woman = new Person("Kate", "Lukosek");
16
17          man.spouse = woman;
18          woman.spouse = man;
19
20          if (man.IsMarriedWith(woman)) {
21              Debug.Log(man.firstName + " is married to " + woman.firstName);
22          }
23          else {
24              Debug.Log(man.firstName + " and " + woman.firstName + " are not married");
25          }
26      }
27  }
28
```

Lines **14** and **15** are calling our newly written custom constructor. As we are instantiating the Person object and assigning firstName and secondName in one line, our code has shrunk by a few lines. This is good! Less code but the same functionality.

 Another good practice in programming is to keep your code as short as possible. If you are able to code the same functionality in fewer lines, you should definitely do it, even if it requires rewriting part of your project.

Summary

Again, well done! Another difficult chapter has been covered. We saw a lot of theory in the first part of the book. Now it's time for more fun. In the next chapter, we will start planning the development of your first Unity game!

8

Let's Make a Game! – from Idea to Development

This chapter will show you how to turn an idea into a ready–to–code project and how to break down complex mechanics into small pieces.

In this chapter, we will cover the following topics:

- Common mistakes made by early developers.
- Breaking a complex idea into manageable parts.
- Pen and paper are your friends. Break the game into features!
- Where you should really start. Fancy game art later, prototype first.
- The core game components (`GameManager`, the `Player`, `Physics`, and the `UI`).
- Target platform, screen resolution, and screen ratio.

Your first game – avoiding the trap of the never–ending concept

When creating your own game, it's a pleasure to finally turn your game idea into reality and be able to play what you imagined, and let your friends play it too. In a way, it is similar to drawing: we have a clear picture in our mind of what we want to draw, and by using a pen and paper we can transmit the picture that we have in our mind into reality. But turning our vision into reality isn't easy at all, especially at the beginning, just like our first drawings, where people were represented by sticks with a circle on top to represent the head.

That is exactly what our first game will look like, simple and unfinished, but to us it will be one of the best games ever made because we created it and it was an amazing experience. The goal is to keep creating games because eventually we will start being good at it, and game after game more people will enjoy them, so don't get discouraged if your first game doesn't look as good as you imagined.

As you are aspiring to become a good game developer, you probably have tons of brilliant ideas for games. If not, you probably have one massive idea that you really want to get done yourself as soon as possible. Maybe you do have some core game mechanics in mind but just don't know how to code it. Good! This book is precisely for you. We will move away from talking about examples and will focus more on coding actual game functionality.

I have spoken to many aspiring game developers who have massive multiplayer games in mind, wanting to create another *World of Warcraft* or *Call of Duty* as their first big project. That's fine! You should think big, and you never know, you might be a part of a great team one day, developing *AAA* titles in Unity. For now, however, we need to take baby steps to get there. That's why we shouldn't think about such massive ideas that take tens of millions of dollars and the most talented teams in the world to develop. We should rather think a bit smaller. You are possibly a one-man team at the moment without a massive budget, but you have a massive passion for game development. Trust me, this is all that you need to release your first game and be *mega proud* of it.

Let's agree to hold on and focus on developing and finishing a simple game in the next few chapters, instead of starting and never finishing something. In this book, we will look at the simple idea of a 2D platform. We will use built-in Unity 2D tools, physics, and, of course, a lot of code.

What do I need to learn before I start creating my own game?

We don't need to learn everything before creating a game. In fact, we can create a fun game just using text. The best advice for your first game is to not complicate it and use what we have learned so far to create a simple game. It doesn't matter whether it works perfectly; it's just an experience. We will have plenty of time to develop all the skills necessary to create a full game from start to finish. For now, just explore.

The concept

Before opening any software, we need to think about the game that we want to create (this process can take a few minutes or can take a few days) until we have a clear picture in our mind about the game that we would like to create. This is the part where we usually don't think about any technical aspects of what we would need in order to create that idea, because we can veto a great idea simply because we don't know how to create it yet. For the purpose of this chapter, our concept will be inspired by a very popular platform game.

The concept of our first game is a 2D platform where the character will go from left to right, avoiding obstacles and enemies, and collecting coins, and to complete it he needs to arrive at the final position.

This is the concept for the game. Now we can imagine it as we want. It can be an easy game or a hard one, the level can be short or long, it can have multiple obstacles and enemies, or just one obstacle repeated throughout the level. Use your imagination to create the level as you please:

This is the game level that I envision, neither extremely easy nor extremely hard, a balanced challenge. So, the idea is for the character to jump on the platforms and avoid falling down the holes. It will have some coins to collect in the harder positions and three checkpoints.

Game mechanics and core components

I want this game to be as simple as possible so that we can complete it in the next few chapters. We will create a lot of scripts, prefabs, and possibly some assets too.

The main mechanics of the game will be as follows:

- The movement of the playable character (run forward, backward, and jump)
- Checkpoints
- Collectable coins
- Obstacles (we could animate some of them)

In most cases, when you have your own idea for a game, you will have a vision in your mind. You will know what sort of feel and gameplay you want to achieve. However, you won't know the tiny parts of the game and how they will work together to create the game you want. This is why planning is so important. Developing the game starts in your head, and then you have to create the documentation for your idea–even if the game is as simple as *Jake on the mysterious planet*. Don't be scared! You may not have to document the complete idea first, but trust me! It's worthwhile to have as much as you can written down.

There aren't any golden rules for game idea documentation. You should aim to write down as much as you want for two main reasons:

- There might be someone else you wish to share your idea with to gather feedback.
- When you write down your idea, you will have tons of new ideas on how to achieve it. Lots of things will pop up in your brain to indicate what could be a good way to do things.

I know what I am saying is very generic, and I am not able to tell you exactly what to do. Your idea is your idea and only you can be successful with it. What I can do, however, is show you how I approach planning.

Breaking the concept into smaller parts

Breaking a project into smaller parts is a general thing to do and can be applied to practically anything, so it's a fundamental step to achieve our goal, which in this case is to create our first game.

We have a very rough idea of what our game will be. The first step will be to divide the game into parts that we can work on independently.

Some of these parts will be as follows:

- Level creation
- The main character's appearance
- Player controls
- The game loop–Start, Game Over, Restart
- Collecting stuff
- Obstacles that kill the player
- The graphical user interface

Depending on our ideas for the game's design, this may vary, but the process will probably be the same. For our example, we need to create the level where the gameplay will happen, the character's or characters appearance and animation, where the player starts and finishes the level, the win and lose conditions, collectible objects, obstacles, enemies that kill the player, the user interface, menus, and checkpoints. There are probably other parts of the game that we will add at a later stage. In fact, this list isn't complete at all, and we will keep updating it whenever a new idea pops up.

Based on this list of the game's core components, we can have some idea about the game. Take a look at this quick sketch. It will give you a much better idea about how this game will work:

For now, we don't need to spend a lot of time drawing. At this stage, all we need to understand is the basic game mechanics. As we can see, our character will be running from left to right, jumping on the platforms, and collecting coins. The main difficulty of this level will be avoiding falling off the platforms. I hope you have an idea now. Yet again, we are making a simple game, but you will learn a lot while developing it.

Testing the mechanics

After deciding how our game will be, we should creating a simple test (without worrying about the design) with only the main features of the game, to see if our idea really works well. By doing this at this stage, we avoid spending a lot of time creating the art of the game, creating the scripts, and putting everything in place because we may end up creating a game that isn't fun, and at least this way we can minimize the amount of work that needs to be redone.

Here we can use simple squares and circles to create our level and add the movement mechanics to an object to test the game.

What's next? Another good step forward is to write down the game's feature list and talk about each of the steps in detail.

Here is the feature list:

- Level design
- An animated 2D character with 2D physics
- Controls
- Collectables and storing the player's data
- A scoring system that stores high scores
- User interface

Let's talk about each of these features to make sure you understand what they are.

Level design

In every game, the level is the key component. It's the environment in which the player moves around and enjoys the game. In this case, we have a classic 2D platform level.

For this game, we will create our own levels, deciding what will happen at each point in the game, creating a challenging and fun experience for the player.

In order to do that, we need to define a few obstacles and platforms that can be placed in the game and the area where the character can walk.

This part of the process we can do first on paper in order to get a general idea of where we want to place the obstacles and platforms. That way, we can have a quick look at what the level will look like. For this example, we used Adobe Illustrator to design our level by using simple squares. Choose the most convenient method for you:

After sketching our level, we can do the same thing in Unity, first by using simple cubes to quickly test our level to see if everything works fine, and then moving forward and adding our assets.

For now, don't worry about planning to code this at all. Remember that we are planning the game. We are not in the active production phase yet. The more you think about the mechanics and how it can work, the better. There will always be a lot of uncertainty while planning, and some solutions that you choose at the planning stage might not work. That's fine! Let's stay open-minded with the game, while at the same time try to plan as much as you can.

An animated 2D character

So, we are creating a 2D game in a 3D game engine. Yes, why not? Unity gives us a lot of brilliant features for creating 2D games. We will use Unity's built-in animation system to animate our character. We will try to add animations for the following:

- Running
- Jumping
- Falling

Physics

For gravity, physics, collision detection, and triggering events, we will use built-in 2D physics components, such as `Rigidbody2D`. As our game is really simple and this book is about learning C#, we will try to keep the physics as simple as possible. In fact, we will just implement gravity and simply check whether our character is on the ground. These two physics mechanics are the absolute minimum for any platform game, and you will be able to reuse most of the code that you write for this.

Mouse and touch controls

We need to give our user a way to control the game. Yet again, simplicity is the key here. I believe we can use the built-in input system and make it universal for standalone platforms and mobile devices. The user will be able to use their mouse and touchscreen. We will possibly use clicks for jump mechanics, and that's it!

Collectables and obstacles

Our character will travel through the level. We will add the ability for them to collect stuff such as coins.

Our character can also be killed by obstacles. To make this work, we will use the built–in Unity physics and write some easy-to-use classes.

Both collecting coins and getting killed by obstacles are initially developed the same way, and that is why we are referring to both actions in the same topic.

If you search in the Unity reference documentation for `MonoBehaviour`, you will find some useful methods called automatically by Unity physics, such as `OnTriggerEnter` and `OnCollisionEnter`. I don't want to go into too much detail on how this will work, but I want you to understand the principle:

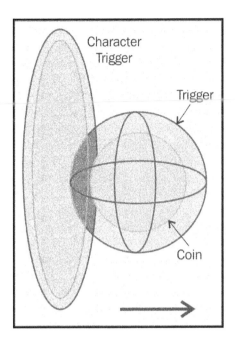

On the left-hand side of the image, we have our character game object. It will contain a `RigidBody` component in order to enable simple gravity physics and physics events.

As soon as the `RigidBody` collider overlaps the coin trigger, the `OnTriggerEnter` method on the `MonoBehaviour` attached to the `RigidBody` game object is executed automatically. I realize that this might feel a bit complicated, so don't trouble yourself about it too much yet. Once we get that far, I will explain it in much greater detail.

Scoring

The main challenge of the game will be completing the levels that we create, but how can we see whether we scored more than our friends? It's simple, we will implement a score; that way, we can compete with our friends or with ourselves, trying to beat our previous record.

For this game, we will be scoring the time in order to find out who has completed the level the quickest, and to do that we will be counting every second and millisecond from the start of the game.

You will learn how to store and retrieve the user's high score.

UI – the user interface

As this book covers the basics, we should first explain what a user interface(UI) is. A user interface is everything on the screen that the user interacts with to control the game. So all buttons, text, and so on are parts of a UI system.

Unity introduced a brilliant UI system with version 4.6. We will focus on the built-in system instead of using a third-party package. Why? Simply because we should learn about the built-in tools that Unity offers.

The game will be divided into a few views, as follows:

- **Main menu view**: This is the first view that the user sees when the game is loaded:

As you can see, the main menu view will be very simple. It will contain only the title, the **Play** button, and the **Quit** button. The **Play** button will take the user to the next view and the **Quit** button will quit the application. We will possibly add a nice background as well, maybe an animated one. Let's keep the background planning open for this view. We can decide on that later.

- **In–game view**: This will be visible during gameplay only:

This is more or less what we want our user to see during the actual gameplay stage. The top-left corner will be occupied by some text. One part of it will say **Score**, and immediately underneath it we will display the current score. The top-right corner will display the highest score ever achieved by the player.

The top center of this view seems to be a good spot for a coin counter. The coin counter will display a coin symbol right next to a text label that shows the currently collected coins. The view won't have a background as it will be filled by the game itself! I hope this makes sense.

- **Game Overview**: This will be shown after the game, when the player character dies:

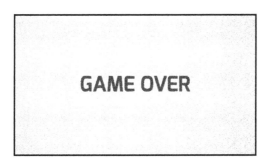

When the player dies, we will move the focus to the Game Overview, most likely displaying the elements shown in the preceding screenshot. A massive **GAME OVER** message will be shown, followed by the score achieved and the count of coins collected. The user will have to make a choice here to either click on **PLAY AGAIN** or go to the **MAIN MENU**:

Target platform and resolution

Unity is a great game engine and allows us to build games on many platforms. One very important stage in the planning of your project is to decide which platforms you would like to support at the beginning. This is simply to find out whether you have any platform-dependent constraints. For example, if you decide to make your game available on mobile phones and tablets, you need to remember that you cannot use mouse right-clicks at all in your game, as you are restricted to using the touchscreen interface. There are many platforms to choose from:

In this book, we will of course go for the easiest option available and choose the **PC, Mac & Linux Standalone** platform.

Target screen resolution

Another good thing to fix at the start is the game's target screen resolution. Unity allows you to create a game that supports dynamic resolution changes. However, we will fix the resolution for now. This will make things easier. Yet again, baby steps forward! We are learning in the right order instead of jumping into deep water.

This is it. Very simple! Almost feels as if it's not worth planning at all? Trust me, it is. The truth is that a game is created in your head first. It's best to take that vision forward and create at least some documentation from it. Make this a rule: note down your ideas as soon as you have them.

Summary

We covered some basic planning in this chapter. It's a very important stage, so try to remember it and don't skip it in your future projects. In the next chapter, we will get this idea going and start turning it into a real Unity project!

9

Starting Your First Game

This is it! We have done some basic planning. Now let's begin the project and build your first game. In this chapter, we will cover the following topics:

- Setting up a new Unity project
- Backing up
- Good practices to keep your project clean
- Preparing the player prefab
- Brief introduction to physics and the `Rigidbody` component
- Collisions and triggers
- Adding a physics force on input
- Update function versus `FixedUpdate`
- First gameplay

Setting up a new Unity project for our game

There are a few basic but important things. Create a new project in Unity. Save it in an easily accessible place. Make sure you have switched the project type to **2D**. It will save us some time while importing assets such as sprites or textures.

There's nothing to worry about here; just make sure you select **2D**, as in the following screenshot:

Backup

Backing up isn't a direct topic in this book; however, I really want to highlight how important this is. Backing up your files will definitely save you from disaster at some point. Lots of things can happen, from hardware failure to rare internal Unity bugs that can ruin your project. That's why it's wise to have a copy of your project somewhere.

I would love to tell you a lot about version control and ways to secure your project. However, version control is a rather advanced topic. We will leave it for now. I recommend zipping your project at least once a day and keeping it in one of the cloud storage services, such as Dropbox or Google Drive.

Keeping your project clean

Organisation is one of the most important aspects if we want to achieve success in our projects, and so before we get into developing our first game, let's take a look at the importance of keeping our project structure clean.

Unity is very flexible in terms of file placement in the Assets folder. This is good, but it can get you into trouble if you overuse it. Let's set up a few rules that we will follow to make sure our project won't end up being messy:

- We'll keep all Assets files inside subfolders and not in the root of the Assets folder
- We'll always name files in the best possible way
- We'll never call any files test; if you are importing a test asset, name it test_xxx, where xxx explains what the file actually contains

Another tip that I can give you is to keep subfolders organized. Have a look at the following screenshot, which shows examples of a bad and good project structure. On the left–hand side of the screenshot, you can see shockingly disorganized files. There are files placed in the root of the Assets folder and different types of files are placed next to each other. On the right–hand side of the screenshot, you can see how I want you to organize your projects. Keep it neat and clean.

You won't regret it when your simple project grows into something bigger that is still easy to manage:

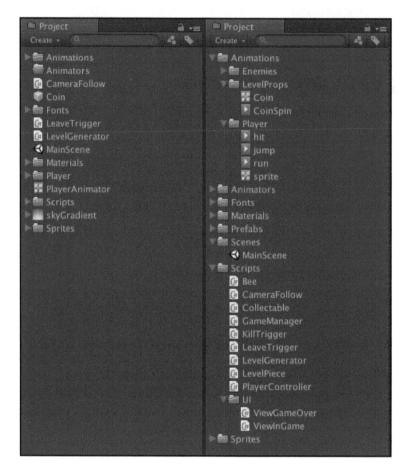

We are ready to start game development now. We have a rough plan, and Unity is set up for the job. Let's finally start now.

Preparing the player prefab

Download the `Player.unitypackage` file. Make sure your Unity Project is open first and then double-click on the `Player.unitypackage` file:

Unity displays a window with the assets we are importing into the project. This contains the necessary files that we prepared for the player character. For now, we'll be focusing on learning about programming the game and not about preparing game art. This is the main reason we will work with prepared assets. We will go through every prefab we are importing to understand how things work. However, you will write the code to control this prefab and create the game!

After clicking on **Import**, you will notice a bunch of folders being created in Unity. We should have the following:

- `Animations`: This folder contains all Unity animation files
- `Materials`: This is for storing all materials and physics materials
- `Sprites`: This is for storing all art sprite assets

Now that we have imported all the necessary files, we can add `Player.prefab` to our scene. It is best if you drag the `prefab` file and drop it on the **Hierarchy** view:

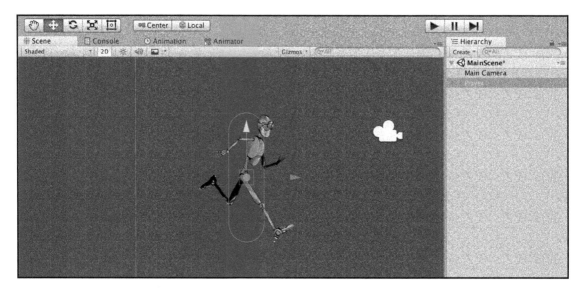

And this is our character, a friendly robot. The first step has been completed, importing the art and animations for the main character of the game, but we don't have any functionality programmed yet. This is our job now: we'll make him run, jump, collect stuff, and, sadly, also die:

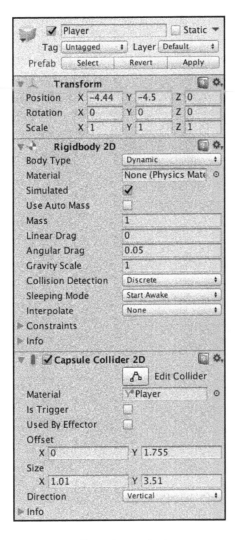

Before we start writing the code, we will go through the components attached to the **Player** game object. Select the **Player** game object and look at the **Inspector** tab.

Let's take a look at the components we have attached to our `Player.prefab`. We'll be deliberately skipping the `Transform` component, as we have already explored this functionality.

Rigidbody2D

According to the Unity manual documentation, a Rigidbody2D component places an object under the control of the physics engine. So simple. We add the `Rigidbody` component to every object we want to enable physics behavior on; for example, in the following image, by adding physics to the other balls, they will react to the impact of the first one.

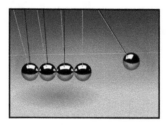

"Computer animation physics or game physics involves the introduction of the laws of `physics` *into a* `simulation` *or* `game engine`*, particularly in* `3D computer graphics`*, for the purpose of making the effects appear more realistic to the observer. Typically, simulation physics is only a close approximation to actual physics, and computation is performed using discrete values."*

– Wikipedia

Once you do that, your `GameObject` will obtain mass and will be affected by gravity. Press **Play** in Unity to see what will happen.

Yes, the robot is falling down endlessly. This is correct, as we don't have any other `GameObjects` (such as the ground) that our character can stand on. We will add soon.

CircleCollider2D

Colliders are necessary for physics objects to affect each other through collisions and triggers. Select the **Player** game object and zoom in on our character that is inside of the **Scene** view. You will see a green circle. This is our 2D collider. The physics engine won't allow any other colliders to overlap with that circle. This means that, if we have a floor, for example, Jake will stand on it!

Let's test this.

Download and import `FloorShort.unitypackage`, drag the newly imported prefab to the scene, and place it underneath our character. Press **Play**, and you will notice that our character will drop and stay on the piece of floor we just imported:

Notice when the colliders meet right under his left leg; this is the collision point. The next step will be to add some functionalities to our character.

PlayerController

This is the moment when we start writing the code for our game. Create a new C# script and call it `PlayerController`. Remember to keep your project structure nice and clean. The wise thing to do is to create a folder called `Scripts` and keep the code there:

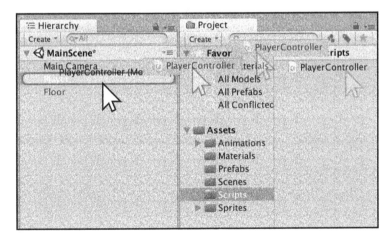

Add the `PlayerController` script to the **Player** game object in our scene by draging and dropping.

User input

The first and relatively the most simple functionality we can add is the ability to jump. We already have basic physics with gravity working on the **Player** game object. Before we can make our **Player** game object jump, we need to know when this should happen. The user always needs some sort of interface in order to interact with the game. On PC and Mac, in most cases, it will be the mouse or keyboard. On mobile devices, it will be the touchscreen.

Unity gives us a lot of *out–of–the–box* functions we can call to check whether the user is trying to interact through any input. For this game, we will be using the keyboard as our main controller. Now let's take a look how to use our keyboard to interact with the game:

```
if(Input.GetKey(KeyCode.Space))
```

As we can see, this is the code that we'll be using to make our keyboard communicate with the game. Here, it says that if we press a key and that key is the space bar, the code that is inside of this statement will run.

For every key, there are three stages of an input:

- `Input.GetKey`:

  ```
  if(Input.GetKey(KeyCode.Space))
  ```

This returns `true` while the user holds down the key identified by name. Think auto fire.

- `Input.GetKeyDown`:

  ```
  if(Input.GetKeyDown(KeyCode.Space))
  ```

This returns `true` during the frame the user starts pressing down the key identified by name. Until you release the key, the code inside of this statement will continue running.

- `Input.GetKeyUp`:

  ```
  if(Input.GetKeyUp(KeyCode.Space))
  ```

This returns `true` during the frame the user releases the key identified by name. The code will only run the moment you release the key.

Now that we understand more about the three stages of an input, we can proceed by choosing the keys that will be responsible for jumping, moving forward, and moving backward.

Jump

Let's take a look at the Unity *Scripting documentation* and search for `scripting reference for Rigidbody2D.AddForce`. This is the way we will apply force to our character. Now we are going to add more code to `PlayerController` so it looks more or less like this:

```
1  using System.Collections;
2  using System.Collections.Generic;
3  using UnityEngine;
4
5  public class PlayerController : MonoBehaviour {
6
7      public float jumpForce = 6f;
8      private Rigidbody2D rigidBody;
9
10     void Awake () {
11
12         rigidBody = GetComponent<Rigidbody2D> ();
13     }
14
15     // Update is called once per frame
16     void Update () {
17
18         if(Input.GetKeyUp(KeyCode.Space))
19         {
20             Jump();
21         }
22     }
23
24     void Jump () {
25
26         rigidBody.AddForce (Vector2.up * jumpForce, ForceMode2D.Impulse);
27     }
28
29 }
30
```

Lots of new code! Let's go through each new line we have added.

Line 7 should be very easy for you to understand now. It declares the `float` type `jumpForce` variable. In lines **8** and **12**, we will be controlling the character physics in the `PlayerController` script, so we need easy access to the `RigidBody2D` component on the same game object.

Have a look at the **Scripting Reference** for `GameObject.GetComponent`. It searches the game object our `PlayerController` is attached to for the `Rigidbody2D` component and returns it so we can assign the `rigidBody` private variable for easy access. `GetComponent` must be called at runtime, so we are calling it in the `Awake` function. After line **12**, we can simply say `rigidBody`. The `RigidBody2D` component will be called on `playerGameObject`.

See how simple the `Jump` function is. It's just a simple line saying, "Hey, RigidBody, apply force with the direction up with this jump force." There are a few force modes we can use for other useful stuff; however, impulse makes sense for jumping. We just want to kick the character up and then let him fall back to the ground.

Go ahead, press **Play** in Unity, and then press the space bar a few times in the game view. We can see that our character is actually jumping, but something is wrong. We need him to jump higher. Experiment with the jump force in the Inspector to find the right value:

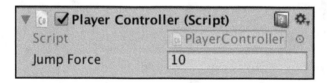

I think the value 10 looks good for the jump height. It's not too high and not too low.

You probably noticed already that we have an issue. We are applying the jump force every time the space bar is pressed. This is good. However, the character should not jump in the air. If you press the space bar many times quickly, he'll simply fly away. We can fix that by adding a bit more code. The right behavior will be to only jump when the character is on the ground.

Let's add the following code and edit the Jump method a little:

```
24    void Jump () {
25
26        if (IsGrounded ()) {
27            rigidBody.AddForce (Vector2.up * jumpForce, ForceMode2D.Impulse);
28        }
29    }
30
31    public LayerMask groundLayer;
32
33    bool IsGrounded() {
34
35        if (Physics2D.Raycast (this.transform.position, Vector2.down, 0.2f, groundLayer.value)) {
36            return true;
37        }
38        else {
39            return false;
40        }
41    }
42
43 }
44
```

I will make a little exception from the rule: I won't analyze this code from top to bottom. I want to talk about the IsGrounded function. In programming and math in general, there isn't a simple way of asking the computer whether the character is on the ground or in the air. When developing a game, one of the main things that we should be able to do is break big and complex ideas into simple programmable parts. Let's not talk about the IsGrounded method yet and focus on line **35**.

Search the scripting reference for Physics2D.Raycast and have a read through. You should see that Raycast is casting a ray against colliders in the scene. To better exemplify what a Raycast is, we'll use a simple real–life example, a laser pointer. Imagine you are holding the laser pointer and pointing at the floor. This is exactly what are we doing in line **35**.

We are basically saying "Hey Unity, shoot the laser down from this `GameObject` position and check whether the distance to hit any object on the ground layer is less than 0.2.":

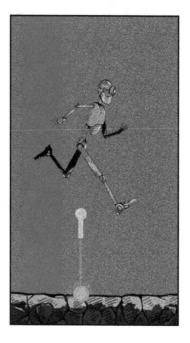

Have a look at this image. The green point represents the origin of the ray we are virtually casting. The blue point is the hit point. The ray distance would be the distance between the origin and the hit point. In this case, we are casting the ray down to a maximum distance of 0.2. I have visualized that distance with an orange line. Looking back at `IsGroundedMethod()`, we can see that the method returns `true` if the raycast hit happens within a distance of 0.2; otherwise, we return `false`.

Let's look at the parameters in the actual `Raycast` function again. `Physics2D.Raycast` has lots of different overloads, which means we can pass a few sets of parameters to the method. In this case, we are using an overload with four parameters:

- `origin`
- `direction`
- `distance`
- `layerMask`

We can preview the names and types of the parameters if we hover our mouse for a few seconds above the word `Raycast` in the code:

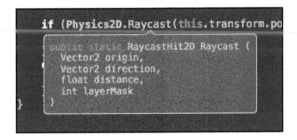

We have already covered `origin`, `direction`, and `distance`. Let's briefly talk about `layerMask`. We can specify a filter here to detect colliders only on certain layers. This means we can set Unity to make `Raycast` work only on specific layers. In this case, we are simply checking whether the **Player** is grounded or not. So, the wise thing to do is to set `Raycast` to work only with objects on the ground layer.

To make sure everything works as it should, we must create the ground layer:

1. In Unity, navigate to **Edit** | **Project Settings** | **Tags & Layers**
2. In the **Inspector**, click on the plus sign and then write `Ground` next to **User Layer**:

3. Select the `Floor` game object in the hierarchy and click on the **Layer** menu:

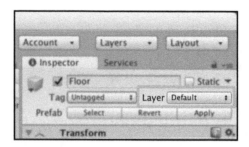

4. Then set its layer to **Ground**. Set it up as shown here:

5. We have the **Ground Layer** set up. Set up the layer mask on the **Player** game object now. If you save the **Player** script, you will notice a new public member variable has appeared:

6. Press **Play** in Unity and perform a test jump. If everything is done correctly, jumping will work only when Jake is on the ground. We check whether our character is on the ground in line **26**. If the `IsGrounded()` method returns `true`, the `Jump` method is called; otherwise, we simply ignore the user input.

Animator

Another important topic in this book is how to animate our character. Certain animations will be played on the character for specific events. Unity has a really clever system already built in for controlling animation: **Mecanim**. We won't go into too much detail about animating stuff in Unity. All I want you to know is that I have prepared the following animation clips for you:

- **Idle**: This is played when the player is not moving (holding position)
- **Run**: This is played when the player is grounded and alive
- **Jump**: This is played during a jump
- **Dead**: This is played when the player hits an obstacle and dies

To preview how animation clips are connected, open the **Animator** view by going to **Window** | **Animator** and selecting the **Player** game object from the hierarchy:

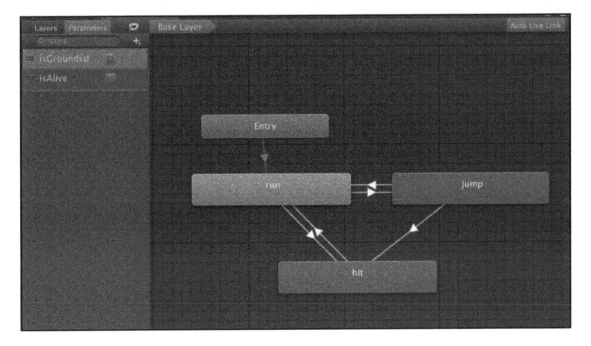

This is an **Animator** view. As we want to focus on programming in this book, we won't discuss the details here. All I want you to notice is the **Parameters** tab and two `bool` type parameters we have already set up. To control animations of Jake, we just need to make sure the `IsGrounded` and `isAlive` bools are set to the correct values. We will do that from our `PlayerController` script.

The first step is to access the **Animator** component in the code. We already learned about the `GetComponent` method of Unity. This time, I want to talk about another way to gain easy access to certain components. Add the following line to your code just after the line that declares the `rigidBody` variable:

```
public Animator animator;
```

Save the script, select the **Player** game object, and look at the **Inspector** panel. We just created a new public member of the **Animator** type and called it `animator`. The **Animator** field will appear in the **Inspector** window. The next step is to assign this variable. Have a look at the hierarchy. There is a child object of the **Player** game object, called `sprite`, we have the **Animator** component on. Simply drag the `sprite` game object from the hierarchy on top of the **None (Animator)** field. Unity will automatically recognize that you are trying to assign **Animator** from the `sprite` game object to the `Animator` variable:

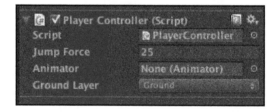

After a correct assignment, the **Inspector** window will look like the preceding screenshot. Now, we have really easy access to the **Animator** component through the `animator` variable within the `PlayerController` script. Let's put that to use. First, set the `isAlive` animator parameter to `true`, as we want Jake to be happy at the start. Add the `Start` method in `PlayerController` with the following line:

```
void Start() {
   animator.SetBool("isAlive", true);
```

At the end of the `Update` method, insert this line to set the `IsGrounded` animator parameter:

```
animator.SetBool("isGrounded", IsGrounded());
```

Save the code and press **Play** in Unity. Jake should be set to the alive state at the start and change his face a little during the jumps. This is cool, isn't it?

Running

Jake is very much alive now–smiling, jumping, and running... in the same place. The next task is to make him run forward. You probably know how we are going to approach this. We can add a constant force forward. Add a `runningSpeed` float public variable to the `PlayerController` class:

```
publicfloat runningSpeed = 1.5f;
```

Also, add the following method to apply the force:

```
31  void FixedUpdate() {
32
33      if (rigidBody.velocity.x < runningSpeed) {
34          rigidBody.velocity = new Vector2(runningSpeed, rigidBody.velocity.y);
35      }
36  }
37
```

The `FixedUpdate` method is called automatically in Unity after a fixed time interval; it is not like the `Update` method, which is called every frame.

`FixedUpdate` is the best place to add constant forces to your physics. If you wish to learn more about the `FixedUpdate` method, dive into Unity's documentation. For now, all you need to understand is that this method is called all the time, and you do not need to call this yourself. In line **34**, we are applying a `Vector2` velocity to the `rigidbody`. The new `Vector2` is a simple C# constructor, and we are passing the x and y values in brackets. Our character is moving from left to right, so we are applying a force with x equal to the running speed and leaving velocity y unchanged.

Line **31** prevents constant acceleration. We are only applying force if the x velocity is lower than the running speed. In other words, if the character's speed is slower than the running speed, push him forward.

Go ahead, save your script and press **Play** in Unity. You will see Jake is moving forward now. We have implemented the running and jumping functionalities. I think we can easily call it our first gameplay! As you have probably noticed, Jake will run forward until he falls off the platform and will be falling forever until you restart. We are missing a game over event here. In the next chapter, we will write the `GameManager` class to help us clamp the whole game functionality together.

Code

This section will cover the code that is present in this chapter.

PlayerController.cs

Here's the code:

```
using UnityEngine;
using System.Collections;

publicclass PlayerController : MonoBehaviour {

  publicfloat jumpForce = 6f;
  publicfloat runningSpeed = 1.5f;
  privateRigidbody2D rigidBody;
  public Animator animator;

  void Awake() {
    rigidBody = GetComponent<Rigidbody2D>();
  }

  void Start() {
    animator.SetBool("isAlive", true);
  }


  // Update is called once per frame
  void Update () {

    if (Input.GetMouseButtonDown(0)) {
      Jump();
    }

    animator.SetBool("isGrounded", IsGrounded());
  }


  void FixedUpdate() {

    if (rigidBody.velocity.x < runningSpeed) {
      rigidBody.velocity = newVector2(runningSpeed, rigidBody.velocity.y);
    }
  }
```

```
void Jump() {
  if (IsGrounded()) {
    rigidBody.AddForce(Vector2.up * jumpForce, ForceMode2D.Impulse);
  }
}

publicLayerMask groundLayer;

bool IsGrounded() {

  if (Physics2D.Raycast(this.transform.position, Vector2.down, 0.2f,
groundLayer.value)) {
    returntrue;
  }
  else {
    returnfalse;
  }
}
}
```

Summary

We finally started actively working on game development. You are doing great. We wrote our basic `PlayerController`, implemented jumping physics, and even discussed triggering animations.

In the next chapter, we will start working on the `GameManager` class, which will allow enclosed game loops.

10
Writing GameManager

We have achieved some basic gameplay. Now is the time to tie it all together. In this chapter, we will cover the following topics:

- What is a `gameplay` loop?
- What is a `singleton` class?
- Writing `GameManager` events?
- Implementing the first game loop

Gameplay loops

Well done so far. You have added basic functionality such as jumping, physics, and running to the `PlayerController` object. We are definitely going in the right direction here. The next important step is writing a neat `GameManager` class to help us control the game events, such as:

- StartGame
- GameOver
- Restart

For basic games such as *Jake on the mysterious planet*, it is a good practice to have one instance of the GameManager running and controlling all main events in the game. The gameplay loop is simply a journey from the gameplay start to the gameplay phase and the game over phase. Time to write some code!

Let's create a new C# script and call it GameManager, and write the following code:

```csharp
using UnityEngine;
using System.Collections;

public class GameManager : MonoBehaviour {


    //called to start the game
    public void StartGame() {

    }

    //called when player die
    public void GameOver() {

    }

    //called when player decide to go back to the menu
    public void BackToMenu() {

    }

}
```

As you can see, nothing is very complicated. We wrote some very simple methods to help us control the main game events. This script does nothing yet; however, please add it to the Unity **Scene**. Create a new game object, call it GameManager, and add the GameManager component to it. We will use it in the future.

We won't test this code in Unity yet. Let's think about what can be improved. Would it be nice to have only one method to control the main events in the game? Let's edit the code a little to have something like that:

```
1   using UnityEngine;
2   using System.Collections;
3
4   public enum GameState {
5       menu,
6       inGame,
7       gameOver
8   }
9
10  public class GameManager : MonoBehaviour {
11
12      public GameState currentGameState = GameState.menu;
13
14
15      void Start() {
16          StartGame();
17      }
18
19      //called to start the game
20      public void StartGame() {
21          SetGameState(GameState.inGame);
22      }
23
24      //called when player die
25      public void GameOver() {
26          SetGameState(GameState.gameOver);
27      }
28
29      //called when player decide to go back to the menu
30      public void BackToMenu() {
31          SetGameState(GameState.menu);
32      }
33
34      void SetGameState (GameState newGameState) {
35
36          if (newGameState == GameState.menu) {
37              //setup Unity scene for menu state
38          }
39          else if (newGameState == GameState.inGame) {
40              //setup Unity scene for inGame state
41          }
42          else if (newGameState == GameState.gameOver) {
43              //setup Unity scene for gameOver state
44          }
45
46          currentGameState = newGameState;
47      }
48  }
49
```

We have an `enum GameState` declaration in lines **4** to **8**. What is `enum`? If you check on Google, you will be probably be directed to the Microsoft documentation. The following is from the C# documentation:

"The enum keyword is used to declare an enumeration, a distinct type that consists of a set of named constants called the enumerator list."

Yes, this is a massively overcomplicated definition. Let's forget it and make our own simple one by defining what we can use `enum` for.

`enum` is a set of magic constants you can control your code with. We can define a few states stored in `enum` and use it without the risk of typos we would have using the string. Lines **4** to **8** simply create a new `enum`, which works like an object and can be passed to the method as a parameter. The rest of the code should be easy for you to understand. `SetGameState` is called with a certain `GameState enum` value. Note that we are also storing the `currentGameState` value for the future.

We have more code that allows us to control events in the game. Now, we need to make some real use of it. If you press **Play** in Unity, you will see that nothing has really changed. Jake still runs the same way he did before `GameManager` was added. This is because nothing actually changed in the `PlayerController` class. `PlayerController` and `GameManager` are two separate instances of two different classes. They won't affect each other's behavior until we write some additional code.

We have already seen how to access components from different scripts by creating a public member variable and dragging the game object to the field in **Inspector**. It is a good approach for this situation. However, I want to show you something better. If there is only one instance of the object required in the project, we can use the singleton approach.

Singleton class

By implementing the singleton pattern for `GameManager`, we can easily access it from anywhere using one single point of access. You probably feel really confused about this now. A simple example will help you get your head around it.

> *"In software engineering, the singleton pattern is a design pattern that restricts the instantiation of a class to one object. This is useful when exactly one object is needed to coordinate actions across the system."*
>
> *– Wikipedia*

Let's add the following code to the `GameManager` class. Declare a new `public static` variable. This code should be written right next to other public variables:

```
public static GameManager instance;
```

Then, add an `Awake` method with the following line:

```
void Awake() {
   instance = this;
}
```

That's it! This is all the code you need for a simple access to the `GameManager` instance from anywhere in your code. It is important to remember that only one instance of this component can be present in the whole Unity **Scene**. To access any of the public code in `GameManager` from another class, you can simply call the following:

```
GameManager.instance.SomeUsefulMethodOrVariable
```

For example, if we want to read the `currentGameState` value from `PlayerController`, we will simply write:

```
GameState currentState = GameManager.instance.currentGameState;
```

I hope the singleton pattern is fairly familiar to you now. Of course, we just covered the basics. Feel free to browse the internet and read more about the subject.

We have easy access to `GameManager`, with basic game events helping to control the game. When we press **Play** in Unity, we can still see that our character is running forward without any control. We are unable to stop him at all. Let's put some restrictions in `PlayerController` so that the running and jumping behavior works only when `currentGameState` is `.inGame`. To do this, let's open `PlayerController` and add some code:

```
void Update () {

    if (GameManager.instance.currentGameState == GameState.inGame)
    {
        if (Input.GetMouseButtonDown(0)) {
            Jump();
        }
        animator.SetBool("isGrounded", isGrounded());
    }

}

void FixedUpdate() {

    if (GameManager.instance.currentGameState == GameState.inGame)
    {
        if (rigidBody.velocity.x < runningSpeed) {
            rigidBody.velocity = new Vector2(runningSpeed, rigidBody.velocity.y);
        }
    }

}
```

Lines **22** and **34** are identical. They contain a simple `if` statement to make the running and jumping functionality work only when `currentGameState` is `inGame`. There isn't much more to explain here. Notice how easily we can access the `currentGameState` due to the singleton approach.

Starting the game

At the moment, our gameplay starts automatically after pressing the **Play** button in Unity. This was convenient for testing running and jumping. If you look into the `Start` method in `GameManager`, you will notice we are calling the start game there. Let's remove that line and keep the `Start` method empty for now.

Further, in the development of this game, we will have a nice **Graphic User Interface** (**GUI**) to control the game states by pressing buttons such as **Start Game** and **Restart**. For now, we should focus on functionality only and leave the GUI for later. However, we do need an easy way to call the events at runtime. Why not use the keyboard for now? You probably remember using `Input.GetKeyDown`. If you don't remember much about it, dive into Unity Scripting Reference again and search for `Input.GetKeyDown`.

Let's say that each time user presses *S* on the keyboard, we will fire up the `StartGame` method on `GameManager`. Before we start adding code, we need to make sure that `currentGameState` is set to `inMenu` just after pressing the **Unity** button. To achieve this, simply edit the `Start` method in `GameManager`:

```
void Start() {
    currentGameState = GameState.menu;
}
```

In Unity, after pressing **Play**, Jake has running and jumping disabled as the current state is `inMenu`. This is how we expect it to work now. Let's add more code to call the `StartGame` method on keyboard press. Write the `Update` method within the `GameManager` class:

```
void Update() {

    if (Input.GetButtonDown("s")) {
        StartGame();
    }
}
```

With your coding experience, you can definitely understand what we are doing here. Every time the *S* button is pressed on the keyboard, the `StartGame()` method will be called.

Setting up input keys

One more thing that's missing now is adding s into Unity's build in `InputManager`. To do that, follow these simple steps:

1. Open **InputManager** by going to **Edit** | **ProjectSettings** | **Input**.
2. Increase the input size of **Axis** by one.
3. Select the bottom **Axis** and change its settings:

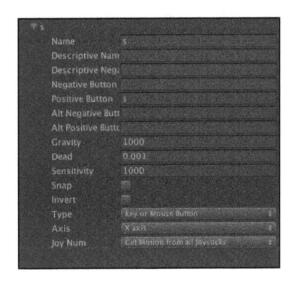

We have a new input button set up and the code that's executed each time the button is pressed. Time to test that. Press **Play** in Unity and, after Jake drops on the platform, press *S* on the keyboard. The `StartGame()` method will be called by Unity just after you press the key. The `StartGame()` method changes `currentGameState` to `inGame`, so our gameplay starts.

So, we have completed the first part of the simple `gameplay` loop. The user can start the game by pressing the button and the game will start. As we are calling it a loop, it will have to be a closed chain of events. To close the gameplay, we will need to add the `GameOver` event.

In our simple game, the game over event will be called when the player dies. There will be two ways to kill the player:

- By falling through the hole in the ground
- By hitting obstacles

We already have the physics functionality working, which means Jake is falling through the holes. All we need to do is create some sort of trigger telling `GameManager` that, "Player has fallen down the hole, game over!"

Using triggers

We can easily configure any collider in Unity to work like a trigger. Triggers are very useful. In this case, we will use them to detect whether our character has fallen into a hole. I have already prepared another useful prefab for you, so we won't waste any time setting it up. The steps are as follows:

1. Import `KillTrigger.unitypackage` into your project.
2. Drag the `Kill` trigger into your project.
3. Position the `KillTrigger` game object so the red area is below the ground:

This is all we need on the **Scene** view. Once Jake drops down from the end of the platform, he will most certainly fall through the red trigger zone. Now, we need to write some code to describe this behavior. It will be a very simple component added to the `KillTrigger` game object.

Create new a C# script, call it `KillTrigger`, and write the code so it looks like this:

```
using UnityEngine;
using System.Collections;

public class KillTrigger : MonoBehaviour {

    void OnTriggerEnter2D(Collider2D other) {

        if (other.tag == "Player") {
            Debug.Log("Player collider entered the trigger");
        }
    }

}
```

As you can see, there is nothing complicated here. We use the `OnTriggerEnter2D` method. It is called automatically by Unity whenever another 2D collider enters the trigger area.

Before we test how things work, we need to make sure our **Player** game object has the correct tag set up. Unity uses tags to help you recognize the game objects in code. It is very useful and easy to use. Select the **Player** game object and set its tag to **Player**:

Now, we are ready to perform a test. Press **Play** in Unity. Then, press *S* on the keyboard to start the game. Our character will start running. If everything works properly, we should get the **Console** message as soon as the character touches the trigger area.

Nice! We can trigger the parts of the code by physics events. Think about different things we can use triggers for, such as collecting stuff. Anyway, at the moment we just call `Debug.Log`. What we really want here is an actual functionality.

Simple logic says that if the player touches the `killTrigger`, the player should die. Let's go back to `PlayerController` and add a new method:

```
public void Kill() {

    GameManager.instance.GameOver();
    animator.SetBool("isAlive", false);
}
```

Before we call this method in `PlayerController`, we need to the change `PlayerController` class into a singleton. We have done this already with `GameManager`. Go ahead and add the `instance` static variable to `PlayerController` and assign it in the `Awake` method. If you feel a bit lost now, go back to the previous part of this chapter where we learned about the singleton approach.

Now we have a really easy `Kill` method to call when something bad happens to our character. Let's go back to the `Kill` trigger and call it instead of `Debug.Log()`. After editing, the `Kill` trigger class should look like this:

```
1  using UnityEngine;
2  using System.Collections;
3
4  public class KillTrigger : MonoBehaviour {
5
6      void OnTriggerEnter2D(Collider2D other) {
7
8          if (other.tag == "Player") {
9              PlayerController.instance.Kill();
10         }
11     }
12 }
13
```

Test the newly written or edited code as soon as possible. Select `GameManager` in the **Hierarchy** first. Press **Play** in Unity and then press the *S* key to start the game. As soon as our character falls into the trigger area, `GameManager.currentGameState` should change from `inGame` to `game over`.

Restarting the game

At this moment, we have a very simple gameplay. We can ask the game to start and we know when the player is finished. All that's missing to complete the game loop is the ability to restart the game.

Restarting the game should be done by the user by pressing the button on the screen or by pressing the button on the keyboard. Let's use the same input event we already have to start the game. The main difference between starting and restarting the game is that actual conditions in the game might be much different. For example, the player's position in the game will be different. In fact, this is a good starting point. Let's make sure every time the game starts, the player's initial position is the same.

Setting up the player starting position

Every time our game starts, we should reset all its conditions to the same state. We already mentioned that resetting the starting position of the **Player** game object would be a good start. Positions in the 3D world in Unity are described using `Vector3 struct`. Go ahead and type `Vector3` in the *Scripting Reference* for a better understanding. This is complex stuff, so don't worry if you can't get it. All you need to know now is that `Vector3` is made up of three floats describing *x*, *y*, and *z* positions in the space.

Let's go forward and perform some code changes to set up the **Player** position. In `PlayerController`, we will do the following:

1. Add a private `Vector3` type variable and call it `startingPosition` in `PlayerController`.
2. Assign the `startingPosition` value taken from the **Player** game object world space position in the `Awake` method. This way, we will always store the initial position of the **Player** game object just after Unity starts executing the game.
3. Rename the `Start` method `StartGame`, as we will call it from the `GameManager` from now.
4. Set the **Player** position to starting position in the `StartGame` method.

Are you feeling a bit confused now? We have carried out a lot of changes in one go. If you really feel lost now, here's what the first part of `PlayerController` should look like (hopefully it will make you less anxious):

```
public class PlayerController : MonoBehaviour {

    public static PlayerController instance;

    public float jumpForce = 6f;
    public float runningSpeed = 1.5f;
    public Animator animator;

    private Vector3 startingPosition;
    private Rigidbody2D rigidBody;

    void Awake() {
        instance = this;
        rigidBody = GetComponent<Rigidbody2D>();
        startingPosition = this.transform.position;
    }


    public void StartGame() {
        animator.SetBool("isAlive", true);
        this.transform.position = startingPosition;
    }
```

Now, inside the `GameManager` `StartGame` method, make sure you are calling:

```
PlayerController.instance.StartGame();
```

```
    //called to start the game
    public void StartGame() {
        PlayerController.instance.StartGame();
        SetGameState(GameState.inGame);
    }
```

As we can see on the image above we have added the line of code under the `StartGame()` void. Now it's time for testing. Save both scripts and come back to Unity. If you are getting any compiler errors, please go back and double-check everything. If you don't have any errors, that's great! Go ahead and press **Play** in Unity. Every time you hit the *S* button on the keyboard, the game will restart and the **Player** game object's position will be set back to its initial position.

Code in this chapter

Here is the code for GameManager.cs:

```
using UnityEngine;
using System.Collections;

public enum GameState {
  menu,
  inGame,
  gameOver
}

public class GameManager : MonoBehaviour {

  public static GameManager instance;
  public GameState currentGameState = GameState.menu;


  void Awake() {
    instance = this;
  }

  void Start() {
    currentGameState = GameState.menu;
  }
  //called to start the game
  public void StartGame() {
    PlayerController.instance.StartGame();
    SetGameState(GameState.inGame);
  }
  //called when player die
  public void GameOver() {
    SetGameState(GameState.gameOver);
  }

  //called when player decide to go back to the menu
  public void BackToMenu() {
    SetGameState(GameState.menu);
  }

  void SetGameState (GameState newGameState) {
    if (newGameState == GameState.menu) {
      //setup Unity scene for menu state
    }
    else if (newGameState == GameState.inGame) {
```

```
      //setup Unity scene for inGame state
    }
    else if (newGameState == GameState.gameOver) {
      //setup Unity scene for gameOver state
    }
    currentGameState = newGameState;
  }


  void Update() {

    if (Input.GetButtonDown("s")) {
      StartGame();
    }
  }

}
```

The following is the code for `PlayerController.cs`:

```
using UnityEngine;
using System.Collections;

public class PlayerController : MonoBehaviour {

  public static PlayerController instance;

  public float jumpForce = 6f;
  public float runningSpeed = 1.5f;
  public Animator animator;

  private Vector3 startingPosition;
  private Rigidbody2D rigidBody;

  void Awake() {
    instance = this;
    rigidBody = GetComponent<Rigidbody2D>();
    startingPosition = this.transform.position;
  }


  public void StartGame() {
    animator.SetBool("isAlive", true);
    this.transform.position = startingPosition;
  }
  void Update () {
```

```
    if (GameManager.instance.currentGameState == GameState.inGame)
    {
      if (Input.GetMouseButtonDown(0)) {
        Jump();
      }
      animator.SetBool("isGrounded", isGrounded());
    }
  }


  void FixedUpdate() {

    if (GameManager.instance.currentGameState == GameState.inGame)
    {
      if (rigidBody.velocity.x < runningSpeed) {
        rigidBody.velocity = new Vector2(runningSpeed,
rigidBody.velocity.y);
      }
    }
  }



  void Jump() {
    if (isGrounded()) {
      rigidBody.AddForce(Vector2.up * jumpForce, ForceMode2D.Impulse);
    }
  }

  public LayerMask groundLayer;

  bool isGrounded() {

    if (Physics2D.Raycast(this.transform.position, Vector2.down, 0.2f,
groundLayer.value)) {
      return true;
    }
    else {
      return false;
    }
  }



  public void Kill() {

    GameManager.instance.GameOver();
    animator.SetBool("isAlive", false);
```

```
      }

  }
```

This is the code for `KillTrigger.cs`:

```
using UnityEngine;
using System.Collections;

public class KillTrigger : MonoBehaviour {
  void OnTriggerEnter2D(Collider2D other) {

    if (other.tag == "Player") {
      PlayerController.instance.Kill();
    }
  }

  }
```

Summary

In this chapter, we covered the basics of the singleton approach. We also covered the gameplay loop. You are doing really well. In the next chapter, we will talk about generating the levels.

11

The Game Level

Let's design a linear level that the player can enjoy.

In this chapter, we will cover the following topics:

- Designed levels versus generated levels
- Creating a level
- Planning LevelGenerator
- Writing LevelGenerator
  - Instantiating random-level pieces at runtime
- Using triggers to create and destroy level chunks

Designed levels versus generated levels

The next big chunk of development in our game is the level. A level is simply the environment that a player is placed in virtually. You are probably a gamer yourself, so I don't really need to explain this much. However, I want to talk about one thing: we need to make a decision on how we want the level to look and behave to keep the player engaged.

A level can be either randomly generated during the game (for example, in *Run*), or have a static, designed by level designer layout (for example, *Super Mario Bros.*).

There are pros and cons to both level types. A designed level can be customized very easily and is easier to develop in general, plus we have full control of the character journey, where he starts, what he needs to do, and where he needs to arrive. This allows us to carefully choose where to place the traps, enemies, or platforms, deciding what should be happening in each part of the game.

If we choose the generating-during-gameplay approach, the level can be endless and random every time the player sees it. The player will always be challenged by different level layouts.

For this example we will be doing a designed level first, that way we can create our own unique levels and choose the difficulty for them and then we will create a generated level so we can play it infinitely.

Let's analyze how a generated level works. We will break it down into a few features of a level, which are as follows:

- A level is made up of level chunks. Each chunk is simply a part of the level.
- Each level chunk will be predesigned.
- The level will be generated by randomly placing the chunks one by one.
- A chunk will be placed in the front of the Player game object and destroyed behind the Player game object.
- Level chunks will be placed seamlessly next to each other so that the player has a feeling of continuous gameplay:

Individual level chunks in the preceding illustration are represented by rectangles with black edges. The section marked in the center of the image is the viewport visible to the player through Unity's camera.

So, in simple words, the player is traveling from left to right. At a later stage, we will make the camera follow the player. When the player game object enters the trigger (the green rectangle), the oldest chunk on the left-hand side will be destroyed (to preserve memory and optimal performance); at the same time, we will instantiate a new chunk in front of the player.

Great! So, this approach gives us an endless level that generates itself, and technically the player can play forever.

Creating a designed level

Now let's start creating our level. Open Unity with the project that we started on Let's Make a Game! From Idea to Development or if you prefer, you can import the Unity package for this chapter that already contains all the necessary files to create the level.

Now let's take a look at the sketch that we have done. The first thing that we will be doing is setting up the floor:

As we can see in the preceding image, the floor has a few empty spaces, and that is what we will be replicating in our game. We already have one object in the `Game Editor` that calls `Floor`, but it is just a small fragment of the whole floor that we need, so it will be necessary to extend it. First, we need to change **Draw Mode** from **Simple** to **Tiled**, as we can see here:

By doing that, we can see that a warning appears, saying that the **Sprite** used is not generated with **Full Rect**:

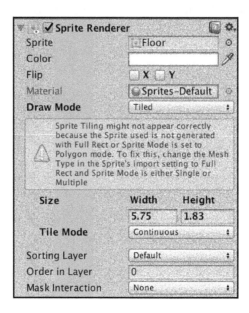

This appears because we did not set the `Sprite` image to be tilled and although it is still possible to use that feature, it might not appear correctly. In order to turn our `Sprite` tilable, we need to go to **Sprite | Inspector** and change **Mesh Type** to **Full Rect** and then click **Apply**:

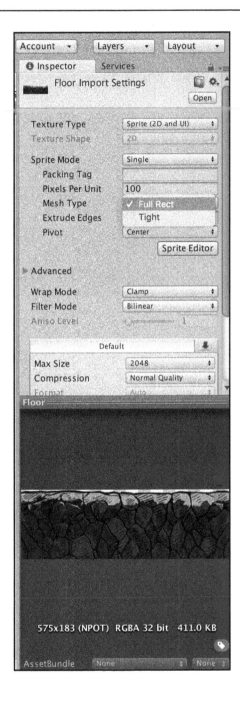

Now the warning is gone and we can change the floor width. For the width size, we have given the value 20, and this piece of floor will represent the first piece that we have sketched. By doing that, we can see that the **Box Collider** does not follow the **Sprite** width, so we also need to change that value:

To fix that, we simply need to set the **X Size** of the **Box Collider** to be the same as our **Sprite**, that in this case is 20:

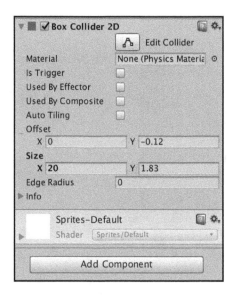

Now that we know how to successfully create a floor with any dimensions we want, we can simply duplicate the `floor` object, move it forward, change the dimensions, and repeat the process until we have completed the level:

So, to create a designed level this is all we need to do for the floor, we choose their size and their position, to make the jumps easier or more difficult. The same process will be applied to the collectibles, obstacles, and enemies of the game, later on we will create them and add them to this level.

Now let's move on to the more complex way of creating a level, by generating chunks of the level that will appear randomly.

Creating a generated level

The level chunk is the most important part of a generated level. It's like a Lego piece. A single piece can't bring about much fun for the player. However, when you take a lot of Lego pieces and fit them together, you can build a structure that's really entertaining. Our level will work exactly the same way. Level chunks right next to each other will create a nice gaming experience (and fun) for the player.

Before we talk about coding the level chunks, we need to make sure that we understand the fundamental parts of each chunk:

This is a level chunk. It can contain whatever you want to add to it. It's up to you to design the chunks. You need to remember, however, that every chunk must have the following features to fit your game:

- **exitPoint–red dot**: This is the point in 3D space where the next chunk will be placed to match this chunk
- **startPoint–green dot**: This is the pivot point of the parent chunk that is plugged into the exit point of the previous chunk
- **exit trigger–green trigger** on the right–hand side: This detects when the player goes through the chunk to tell `LevelGenerator` to destroy the old piece and instantiate a new piece
- **kill trigger–red box**: This is an optional trigger that kills the player on contact

So, this is it! A very simple part of a level that we call a level chunk. Let's do something exciting now and write a procedural level generation.

Planning the LevelGenerator class

Remember that we are not writing any code without quick planning. Let's quickly think about the `LevelGenerator` script and the functionality.

We will definitely need to write methods for:

- `AddPiece`: which is the level chunk right behind the last level chunk that is already generated
- `RemoveOldestPiece`: to keep Unity clean of already–used level chunks
- `RemoveAllPieces`: to cleanse the level of all chunks
- `GenerateInitialPieces`: to generate a few pieces straight away when the game starts

Beforewe get to coding, let's prepare some assets.

Download and import `LevelPieceBasic.unitypackage`into your project. You will notice that the`PlayerPieceBasic`prefab has been imported into the prefabs folder. Drag this prefab into the **Hierarchy** window. Make sure that the entire`PlayerPieceBasic`game object in the **Scene** is placed on `GroundLayer`. Otherwise, the`Player`script won't detect that the player is on the ground. If we get this wrong, the player won't be able to jump.

At this stage, we will have quite a disorganized project hierarchy. It might be worth giving it a little cleanup. We won't use the `FloorShort` and `KillTrigger` game objects for a while, so let's delete them. Our **Hierarchy** and **Scene** windows should look more or less like this now:

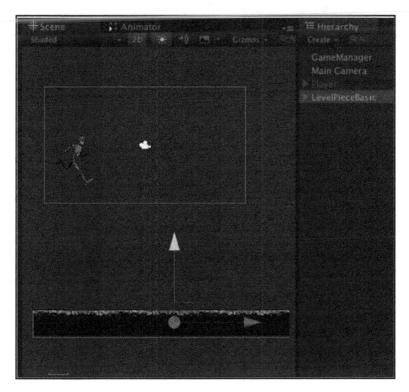

Let's take a look at the prefab we just imported. As you can see, there is nothing fancy here. It's just a straight floor piece without any obstacles or holes. It's perfect for a start.

If you look closely at what's inside `LevelPieceBasic`, you will notice a very simple structure, as we have mentioned before. There are lots of individual floor pieces, `ExitPoint`, and `LeaveTrigger`. At the moment, we don't have any scripts attached to them.

The key element for generating the level is knowing the position where the elements will appear. We will use the `ExitPoint` world space position for this. I understand that this might sound a bit confusing again. Let's write a very simple piece of code that we will use to manage the `LevelPiece` and hold the reference to the `ExitPoint` game object.

Create a new C# script, call it `LevelPiece`, and add the `exitPoint` `public` member, as shown here:

```
using UnityEngine;
using System.Collections;

public class LevelPiece : MonoBehaviour {

    public Transform exitPoint;

}
```

That's it! No complicated code here! We are using the `LevelPiece` component just to hold the `ExitPoint` transform reference.

Add the `LevelPiece` component to the `LevelPieceBasic` game object, and assign `ExitPoint` by dragging and dropping the `ExitPoint` game object on top of the slot, as shown in this screenshot:

We are just about to build the `LevelGenerator` class that will spawn level pieces in the level. The `LevelPiece` class will help us manage the pieces that are already in the game and will massively speed up their positioning correctly through the `ExitPoint` reference.

Writing the script LevelGenerator

We are ready to start writing the level generator. Woohoo! But before we proceed, let's have a recap of what functionality we have planned to include.

We will need to write methods for the following:

- AddPiece: the level chunk right behind the last level chunk that is already generated
- RemoveOldestPiece: to keep Unity free of already used level chunks
- RemoveAllPieces: to clean up the level of all chunks
- GenerateInitialPieces: to generate few pieces on the game start straight away

Let's create a new script and call it LevelGenerator. Let's also change the way we talk about new code here. As LevelGenerator is quite an important class, I want you to understand it fully. That's why we will talk about variables as of now. Later, we will move on to methods.

Now add the following code to LevelGenerator:

```
using UnityEngine;
using System.Collections;
using System.Collections.Generic;

public class LevelGenerator : MonoBehaviour {

    public static LevelGenerator instance;
    public List<LevelPiece> levelPrefabs = new List<LevelPiece>();
    public Transform levelStartPoint;
    public List<LevelPiece> pieces = new List<LevelPiece>();

    void Awake() {
        instance = this;
    }

}
```

As we can see in line **7**, we are declaring a static variable. You already know that we need this static variable for easy access using the singleton approach.

The Game Level lines **8**, **9**, and **10** declare some useful variables:

- levelPrefabs: This is the list of all already prepared level pieces. We will store all different level pieces that we want the generator to copy from.
- levelStartPoint: This is a transform. We will plug in a game object in the scene that we will use to describe where the level is starting. In simple words, this is the position of the very first level piece in the level.
- pieces: This is another list of level pieces. We will use this variable to store all level pieces that are in the game at the time.

What is the difference between the `levelPrefabs` and `pieces` variables? Basically, the `levelPrefabs` elements are our `blueprints`. Every time we ask the generator to add a new piece to the level, the generator will randomly pick one prefab (`blueprint`), make a copy of it, place it in the scene, and add this copied level piece at the end of the pieces list. So, remember that the `levelPrefabs` list won't change during the gameplay. The `pieces` list, however, will constantly change as the player progress through the level.

Creating a copy of the level piece

We are now ready to write a clever method that will copy `levelPrefab` and place it at the right location on the level.

Add the following method to the `LevelGenerator` class:

```
public void AddPiece() {

    //pick the random number
    int randomIndex = Random.Range(0, levelPrefabs.Count);

    //Instantiate copy of random level prefab and store it in piece variable
    LevelPiece piece = (LevelPiece)Instantiate(levelPrefabs[randomIndex]);
    piece.transform.SetParent(this.transform, false);

    Vector3 spawnPosition = Vector3.zero;

    //position
    if (pieces.Count == 0) {
        //first piece
        spawnPosition = levelStartPoint.position;
    }
    else {
        //take exit point from last piece as a spawn point to new piece
        spawnPosition = pieces[pieces.Count-1].exitPoint.position;
    }

    piece.transform.position = spawnPosition;
    pieces.Add(piece);
}
```

When creating procedurally generated levels, we want to make sure that the level is different every time the player sees it. For our solution, we simply want to pick a random element from the `levelPrefabs`.

Please take a look at Unity's reference and search for `Random.Range`. You will realize that `Random.Range` returns a randomly generated number that lies between two numbers (`min` and `max`).

So, if we use `Random.Range`, passing `0` and the count of all level prefabs, we have at our disposal a random integer number. We can use this number as an index from the `levelPrefabs` list. This is exactly what we are doing in line **33**.

Great! Now we know how to generate a random number to help us pick the right `levelPrefab` to copy and add to the level.

Instantiating

I have used the word `Instantiate` a few times before. What does it mean? Instantiating simply means creating a copy of the object. Yet again, I encourage you to go back to the **Scripting Reference** and read about `Instantiate`.

Line **36** is where we are using Instantiate:

```
LevelPiece piece = (LevelPiece)Instantiate(levelPrefabs[randomIndex]);
```

In this line, we are creating a copy of one of the `levelPrefabs` elements stored under the `randomIndex` value. We assign the instantiated object straight away to the local piece variable. So basically, this is the line that creates an exact copy of the prefab and places it in the scene.

When instantiating a game object, we are creating a copy of the object. Unity, however, doesn't copy its parent assignment, so the instantiated object will be created on top of the hierarchy. To correct this, we set the parent to the piece object using the `transform.SetParent` function on line **37**.

Great! We know how to create a copy of a game object and assign a parent to it. The next step is to position the newly created level piece at the right place in our level. Let's try to understand the rest of the `AddPiece` function line by line.

Vector3

As you know Unity a bit, have you heard of Vector3 already? If you haven't, I will explain it very briefly. Vector3 represents a 3D vector and a point or direction. The Unity documentation says:

> *"This structure is used throughout Unity to pass 3D positions and directions around. It also contains functions for doing common vector operations."*

Feel free to learn more about Vector3 at :
`http://docs.unity3d.com/ScriptReference/Vector3.html`. If you are not a math master, you will feel confused now. All I want you to remember right now is that Vector3 can be used to store the position of a game object in 3D space. It contains the *X*, *Y*, and *Z* positions in 3D space. That's it! Don't bother yourself with too much information about 3D vectors at this stage; it is a massive subject.

Line **39** is where we are creating a new Vector3 type variable to store the position we will move our level position to in the next few lines.

 You can use `List<T>.Count` to access the current size of the list. `List<T>.Count` returns an `int` value.

The `if` statement on line **42** checks whether the piece we are adding to the level is the very first piece in the level. If this statement is `true`, then line **44** is executed, assigning the `levelStartPoint.position` value to the `spawnPoint` local variable.

In other words, if the `pieces` list count is 0, it means that we are adding the very first piece to the level, and its position will be the same as that of the `levelStartPoint` variable.

If we do not add the first piece to the level, the `piece.Count` value will be different from 0 and line **48** will be executed instead of line **44**.

It is crucial that you understand fully how line **48** works. In this line, we are assigning the value to `spawnPoint`. What value? That's a good question. To get the position, we are looking back into the `pieces` list–at the last element stored in that list. The last element in the `pieces` list will always be the last level piece that is already placed in the level, so we can use the `exitPoint.position` value here. Remember the `LevelPiece` class? The `ExitPoint` is the position where the next piece will connect to; you learned about this a few pages back.

Great! So at this point, we know that the `spawnPosition` value should be set to either the initial position from which the level starts or the exit point of the last piece in the level. All that we need to do now to make the newly spawned piece jump to the right position is assign its `.transform.position` value. We do that in line **51**. Line **52** adds the new piece to the list for easy access.

This was a tough phase in the game. I really hope you don't feel confused now. Don't worry too much if you do. Things will be much clearer when you see your `LevelGenerator` working in the **Scene** view.

Chapter 11

Testing LevelGenerator

We went through some difficult coding recently. You might feel a bit uncomfortable still, but don't worry. The more time you spend coding, the more confidence you gain.

To test whether everything works correctly, we need to do some setup in the **Scene**:

1. Create a new `GameObject` and call it `LevelGenerator`.
2. Add a `LevelGenerator` Component to the `LevelGenerator` game object.
3. Create a new game object and call it `startPoint`.
4. Position the start point game object in the scene so that it is below and behind the `Player` game object. Thus, the first generated level piece will appear directly under the `Player`.
5. Assign the `LevelPieceBasic` game object as the first element on the `LevelPrefabs` array.
6. Assign the `startPoint` game object into the correct slot in the `LevelGenerator` component:

7. Ready to test? Click **Play** in Unity. If all goes well, you should see two initial level pieces generated.

Congratulations! You just wrote a working part of a procedurally–generated level. I get it's not the most exciting level yet. We will slowly get there; don't worry! Press *S* on the keyboard to start the game.

Extending the level

At the moment, our character moves forward and eventually will run to the edge and drop. To avoid this, we will simply generate the next piece of the level every time the player leaves one level piece behind. We will also destroy the *old* and already used piece of level to keep things clean.

We will use the `OnTriggerEnter` method to recognize when the player reaches the `ExitTrigger` of a certain level piece:

```
58   public void RemoveOldestPiece() {
59
60       LevelPiece oldestPiece = pieces[0];
61
62       pieces.Remove(oldestPiece);
63       Destroy(oldestPiece.gameObject);
64   }
65
```

First things first, we need to make sure that our level generator contains the functionality needed to extend the level. Let's add the `Remove OldestPiece void` method to the level generator.

With your coding experience, you should easily understand line by line what we are doing in this method. If you don't, just remember that this method will remove the oldest `levelPiece` from the level.

We are getting closer to a working endless level. The last piece of the puzzle is calling the `AddPiece` and `RemoveOldestPiece` methods when the `Player` game object enters the trigger.

Let's write one more component that we will add to the `LeaveTrigger` game object in every `LevelPiecePrefab`. Create a new C# script and call it `LeaveTrigger`:

```
1  ⊟ using UnityEngine;
2  └ using System.Collections;
3
4  ⊟ public class LeaveTrigger : MonoBehaviour {
5
6  ⊟      void OnTriggerEnter2D(Collider2D other) {
7
8              LevelGenerator.instance.AddPiece();
9              LevelGenerator.instance.RemoveOldestPiece();
10     └      }
11
12 └ }
```

The `OnTriggerEnter2D` method is called automatically by Unity whenever `RigidBody2D` enters the 2D collider. If you look closely at the `Player` game object, you will see that one of its components is a `Rigidbody`. Where is our trigger then? We actually have a game object called `LeaveTrigger` as a child of `LevelPieceBasic`. In theory, we have all the parts needed for the `OnTriggerEnter2D` method to be called on the `LeaveTrigger`.

Add the `LeaveTrigger` component to the `LeaveTrigger` game object and click **Play** in Unity.

What should happen? After you press *S* to start the game, our character will start running through the level. As soon as he enters the `LeaveTrigger` game object, we will call the `AddPiece` method to extend the level and the `RemoveOldestPiece` method to clean up the oldest piece in the level.

Please note that you can observe level generation only in the scene view. Why? Because the **Main Camera** we are using to render what is happening is in a static position right now. We will add a smart script to the camera very soon to make it follow the `Player` game object:

1. Download `CameraFollow.unitypackage` from the Packt hub and import it to your project
2. Add the `CameraFollow` component to the **Main Camera** game object
3. Drag the `Player` game object into the **Target** slot in the **Camera Follow** component, as shown in this screenshot:

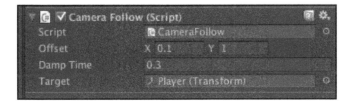

The code used in this chapter

Here are the pieces of code used in the chapter:

The code for `LevelPiece.cs`:

```
using UnityEngine;
using System.Collections;

public class LevelPiece : MonoBehaviour {

  public Transform exitPoint;

}
```

The code for `LevelGenerator.cs`:

```
using UnityEngine;
using System.Collections;
using System.Collections.Generic;

public class LevelGenerator : MonoBehaviour {

  public static LevelGenerator instance;
  //all level pieces blueprints used to copy from
  public List<LevelPiece> levelPrefabs = new List<LevelPiece>();
  //starting point of the very first level piece
  public Transform levelStartPoint;
  //all level pieces that are currently in the level
  public List<LevelPiece> pieces = new List<LevelPiece>();
  void Awake() {
    instance = this;
  }

  void Start() {
    GenerateInitialPieces();
  }


  public void GenerateInitialPieces() {
    for (int i=0; i<2; i++) {
      AddPiece();
    }
  }
  public void AddPiece() {

    //pick the random number
```

```
    int randomIndex = Random.Range(0, levelPrefabs.Count-1);

    //Instantiate copy of random level prefab and store it in piece
variable
    LevelPiece piece = (LevelPiece)Instantiate(levelPrefabs[randomIndex]);
    piece.transform.SetParent(this.transform, false);

    Vector3 spawnPosition = Vector3.zero;

    //position
    if (pieces.Count == 0) {
      //first piece
      spawnPosition = levelStartPoint.position;
    }
    else {
      //take exit point from last piece as a spawn point to new piece
      spawnPosition = pieces[pieces.Count-1].exitPoint.position;
    }
    piece.transform.position = spawnPosition;
    pieces.Add(piece);
  }



  public void RemoveOldestPiece() {
    LevelPiece oldestPiece = pieces[0];
    pieces.Remove(oldestPiece);
    Destroy(oldestPiece.gameObject);
  }

}
```

The code for LeaveTrigger.cs:

```
using UnityEngine;
using System.Collections;

public class LeaveTrigger : MonoBehaviour {


  void OnTriggerEnter2D(Collider2D other) {

    LevelGenerator.instance.AddPiece();
    LevelGenerator.instance.RemoveOldestPiece();
  }
}
```

Summary

Great! We now have all of the functionality we need for the designed level and for the infinite gameplay. You just learned how to create reusable pieces of a level. You also learned how to populate the level pieces to create an illusion of an endlessly running game. In the next chapter, we will explain how to construct and implement a user interface for our game.

12

The User Interface

Now that we know how to design a level and make it playable, it is time to introduce a **User Interface** (**UI**) into our game. We will construct and implement a simple, dynamic UI using Unity's built-in UI system.

But what is a UI? As the name suggests, a user interface is the text, images, or animations that we can see on top of our game; it is a bridge between a human and a computer program, practically all the graphical elements that the user can interact with to control the game or to get information from it. For example, virtual buttons that we can see displayed on mobile games are part of the UI, and the text that shows us the number of coins that we have collected is also part of the UI.

For our game, we need a few UI elements to make it more interesting and to give it a purpose, because without any graphics we don't know how many coins we have collected, how much time we have left, or whether we have broken our previous record.

So in this chapter, we will cover the following topics:

- Introducing the Unity UI
- Creating UI views
- Connecting buttons to actions
- Switching UI views

So far, our sole focus has been on learning how to code. I would like to make a little exception in this chapter and talk about coding the UI functionality, as well as creating a good-looking UI.

Introducting the Unity UI

Unity UI is the component responsible for all the graphics that are displayed on top of the game. It is like a separate layer where we can add images, animation, or text that through code are linked to what is happening inside the game, although it is also possible to create a full game by only using this component. With this in mind, we can see already that a lot of things are possible to create using Unity UI, but for now let's focus on the principles and learn how to create the basic interfaces, making sure that everything we do is functional before adding more features.

Views

From now on, we will be using the term *view* a lot. In simple words, a view is a portion of the application's UI that is visible to the user at a particular time:

- Our simple game will contain three simple views: the **Menu** view, the **InGame** view, and the **GameOver** view
- Each view will contain all UI elements, such as buttons and labels
- Only one view can be displayed to the user at a time

Constructing the view UI – how to keep things clean

To draw UI elements, Unity requires a game object with the **Canvas** component on it. Every time we add a UI element, it will be added inside of an existing Canvas or it will create a new Canvas (inside the `Hierarchy Panel`).

We will start with the Menu view, and here we will have only a **Play** button. The Menu view is the first view that the user will see after they launch our game. Follow these steps:

1. Create a new game object and call it `UI`. It will be a root of our UI, which means that all views and UI elements will be children of this view. This will help keep the UI and the actual game separate.
2. Create a new child game object and call it `MenuCanvas`.
3. Add a Canvas component to the `MenuCanvas` game object with the following settings:

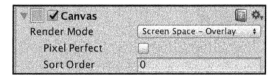

The **Canvas** component represents the abstract space in which the UI is laid out and rendered. All UI elements must be children of a `GameObject` that has a **Canvas** component attached.

The reason we chose **Screen Space – Overlay** in **Render Mode** is that it does not require an additional camera. As we are trying to keep our first Unity game as simple as possible, this is an obvious choice.

4. Add the **Canvas Scaler** component to the `MenuCanvas` game object with these settings:

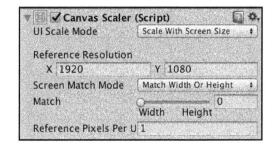

The **Canvas Scaler** component is used to control the overall scale and pixel density of UI elements on the **Canvas**. This scaling affects everything on the **Canvas**, including font sizes and image borders. Yet again, to keep things simple, we will pick the easiest scaling mode, **Scale With Screen Size**.

Target screen resolution

One important aspect that we need to take into consideration when designing the UI is deciding what screen resolutions and aspect ratios we want to support. Currently, modern games support multiple screen resolutions in order to support a variety of games, monitors, and touchscreen devices because that way we can export to multiple devices without changing our UI. For this example, we will stick to the easiest solution and choose a static canvas resolution of 1920 pixels by 1080 pixels.

Recognizing events

All interactions with the UI occur through the **Event System**. Actions such as button clicks, drag–and–drop UI elements, and swipe gestures require the Event System to be present in the Unity scene all the time.

The Event System is a way of sending events to objects in the application based on the input, whether a keyboard, mouse, touch, or custom input.

To add the Event System to our game, we simply navigate to **GameObject** | **UI** | **Event System:**

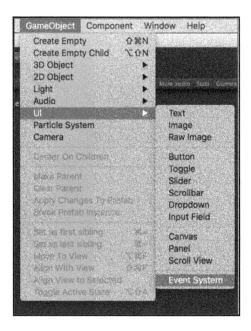

When you add an **Event System** component to a GameObject, you will notice that it does not have much functionality exposed. This is because the **Event System** itself is designed as a manager and facilitator of communication between **Event System** modules.

We are missing one more component in the view. Add the **Graphic Raycaster** component to the **Menu Canvas** game object. The raycaster looks at all graphics on the canvas and determines whether any of them have been hit.

Great! Our **MenuCanvas** contains all the elements necessary to render and allow user interaction with UI elements.

Our **MenuCanvas** game object should look like this:

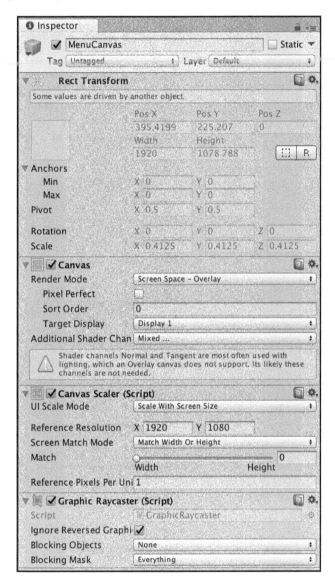

Buttons

One of the most common UI elements is a simple button. Pretty much all UI interfaces on the most commonly available Unity platforms contain buttons. The simplest interaction with a button is a click. You will now learn how to construct a button in Unity UI and call a certain method in the code when the button is clicked on.

To speed up your learning process, I have prepared ready–to–use UI elements.

Download and import `MenuViewUIElements.unitypackage` into your Unity project.

Unity will import a few useful assets with this package. In the **Project** view, find `Prefabs/UI/PlayButton.prefab` and drag it directly on top of the Menu Canvas, as shown here:

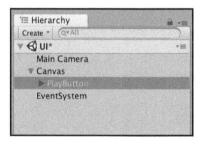

Also, do the same for `Prefabs/UI/QuitButton.prefab`. After dropping the prefabs, the **PLAY** and **Quit** buttons should appear on the canvas, like this:

Basic button

Even a basic button contains a few components, and for that reason it is important to learn about all the main functionalities of a button before creating one. First, we will talk about the visual parts that make up the simple labeled button, the **image**.

The image

Unity can draw 2D images on the UI canvas. Select your button and take a look at the **Inspector** window:

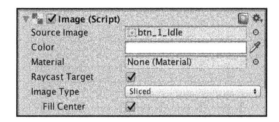

We are using the **Image** component on our button to give it a visual presence. In simple words, the **Image** component gives our button a background.

The Button component

The actual interaction with the button is controlled by the **Button** component:

The **Button** control responds to a click from the user and is used to initiate or confirm an action.

Interaction

This is our first button. Although it might not look very impressive, it's functional. To check how it works, click on **Play** in Unity and press the button in the game view.

At this stage, nothing will happen yet. But we can observe that the button is visually changing a little when you click on it:

Now we need to assign an action to the button to call the part of code that we need.

All user interaction with Unity UI is driven by events. The button has one type of event already built into its component. It is the simple `OnClick` event:

The `OnClick` event is invoked when a user clicks on the button and releases it. At the moment, the list of methods that we want to invoke when the `OnClick` event happens is empty. That is why the button isn't doing anything useful. Let's hook it up with a method and see how it works.

The Button action

Unity's Event Systems are very flexible. The `OnClick` event allows you to call any public method in your code directly from the **Button** component. Follow the few simple steps given here to assign a specific method in the code that you want to call when the UI button is clicked on by the user:

1. Select the game object containing the **Button** component.
2. Press the + button in the **Event** section, as shown here:

3. Drag and drop the `GameObject` containing the script with the `public` method you want to call from the event. In this case, it is the `GameManager` game object. Drop `GameManager` into the **Object** field:

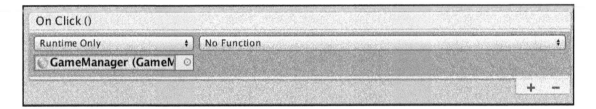

4. From the function list, select the component name and then the method name of the function that you want to be called when the button is clicked on. Since we are creating the **Play** button, we will call the `StartGame()` function from `GameManager`, as shown here:

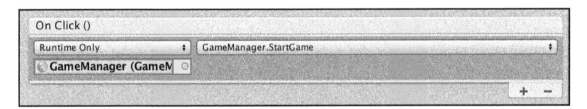

 If you cannot see your function on the function list, it probably means that `EventSystem` cannot access the function as it is private. Change the access modifier to `public`.

We now have all the bits and pieces we need for the button to work. We have set up the **Canvas** view to render UI elements. We have an `EventSystem` to process and trigger events caused by the user. And we also have the first event called when the user presses the **Play** button.

Let's test the **Play** button! Press **Play** in Unity and click on the green **Play** button in the Game view.

It's working! As soon as you press the **Play** button, the Event manager will invoke the `StartGame()` function, which is under `GameManager`, and the game will start.

The button is working great. However, something is not right. The user will expect the menu to disappear just after they've pressed the button. Let's get this sorted right away.

Hiding and showing the Canvas

We have decided that the UI in our game will be made up of three simple views:

- MenuView
- InGameView
- GameOverView

We have created most of the MenuView. I am using two terms here, View and Canvas. In our simple game, both of them will mean the same thing. MenuCanvas is just the visible part of MenuView. Keep that in mind.

The simplest way to toggle the view's visibility is by enabling and disabling the **Canvas** component. Let's test how it works without the code for now:

1. Press **Play** in Unity.
2. Select the **MenuCanvas** game object in the **Hierarchy** window.
3. Disable the **Canvas** element, marked here:

4. As the **Canvas** component is responsible for rendering the UI in the scene, disabling it will hide the content of all UI elements within the canvas.

Note once again that disabling the **Canvas** component will hide all UI elements within the canvas. It will also disable all events handled by the Event System.

It's been a while since we wrote some code. Let's implement the same behavior in the code. Add a Canvas type public member to the GameManager class and call it menuCanvas. We will use this reference in GameManager for easy access:

```
public Canvas menuCanvas;
```

Edit `SetGameState` by adding three lines that enable and disable the **Canvas** component, as follows:

```
void SetGameState (GameState newGameState) {

    if (newGameState == GameState.menu) {
        //setup Unity scene for menu state
        menuCanvas.enabled = true;
    }
    else if (newGameState == GameState.inGame) {
        //setup Unity scene for inGame state
        menuCanvas.enabled = false;
    }
    else if (newGameState == GameState.gameOver) {
        //setup Unity scene for gameOver state
        menuCanvas.enabled = false;
    }

    currentGameState = newGameState;
}
```

Well done! We have a piece of basic code that enables and disables the **Canvas** for us.

Reference exceptions

Test the code by pressing **Play** in Unity and then clicking on the **Play UI** button. The `SetGameState` function that we just added to `GameManager` should hide the `MenuCanvas`. Oops! Something is wrong. Unity is displaying an error in the **Console** window. Something surely went wrong. Let's take a look at the red error message, which is shown here:

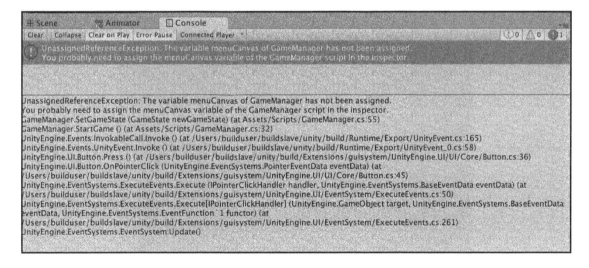

In your programming career, you will come across many issues with the games or applications that you are creating. I have deliberately asked you to follow my steps to cause this issue. We will learn with experience. Beginners in programming often rely on luck while sorting out issues. They blindly change something, test again, and keep going in that loop until they fix the issue by pure luck, or simply give up on trying. This is a very bad approach to debugging. I want you to understand what the issue is. In most cases, Unity will try to give you an accurate description of the error in the Console. Once we face an issue, we will learn to understand what's wrong, and only then will we be able to fix the code issues. While learning something new, we will gain experience and write flawless code.

Let's take a look at the **Console** window again. As you can see, the console is divided into two sections:

- **The top section**: This displays all error and warning messages, usually with a short description
- **The bottom section**: This has a full description of an error or warning, with the stack trace message showing the sequence of nested functions called up to this point

Our error says: **UnassignedReferenceException: The variable menuCanvas of GameManager has not been assigned. You probably need to assign the menuCanvas variable of the GameManager script in the inspector.**

Hmm... To see the exact line that is throwing up the error, double-click on the error in the Console. MonoDevelop should open after a few seconds, selecting the line that is causing the issue:

```
void SetGameState (GameState newGameState) {

    if (newGameState == GameState.menu) {
        //setup Unity scene for menu state
        menuCanvas.enabled = true;
    }
    else if (newGameState == GameState.inGame) {
        //setup Unity scene for inGame state
        menuCanvas.enabled = false;
    }
    else if (newGameState == GameState.gameOver) {
        //setup Unity scene for gameOver state
        menuCanvas.enabled = false;
    }

    currentGameState = newGameState;
}
```

The selected line is causing the issue

> Double–click on the error in the Console. It will open up `MonoBehaviour` and highlight the exact line that is causing the issue.

We are not asking Unity to do much in this line. What we are trying to do is set the **Canvas** component stored under the `menuCanvas` variable name to `false`. What can go wrong then? An unassigned reference exception means Unity is trying to use a variable that is not properly assigned. I led you to this issue deliberately, as this is a very common mistake made by beginner programmers.

Still confused? Not sure what I mean? Select the `GameManager` game object and take a look at your `GameManager` component in the inspector, as follows:

It should be clear to you now. We forgot to connect the **Menu Canvas** slot with the `MenuCanvas` game object. To fix this, simply drag and drop the `MenuCanvas` game object into the **Inspector**, just as you did before.

Make sure that the **Clear on Play** toggle in your **Console** is switched on. Press **Play**. The error should disappear and everything should work as expected.

Great! We have created a Menu view with a simple, fully working button. The Menu view will be the first view seen by our user. It would be good to include a game name in this view.

Download and import `GameLogo.unitypackage` from the Packt hub. The `GameLogo` prefab will be imported into the `Assets/Prefabs/UI` folder. Simply drag and drop this prefab onto the `MenuCanvas` game object.

A very simple game logo will appear on the Menu Canvas!

Feel free to change the name of the game and anything else you wish. Hey! At the end of the day, this is your game, right!

GameView

It's a great time to add more UI to the game! I have prepared the second one for you–InGameCanvas. Yet again, you have to download and import InGameCanvas.unitypackage.

Import the aforementioned package and drag the newly created InGameCanvas.prefab file on top of the UI game object.

InGameCanvas should appear as a child of the UI game object. It will be invisible for now, but don't worry about it too much at the moment. We will need to add a bit of code to manage the visibility of InGameCanvas and MenuCanvas.

As I have mentioned before, the plan is to show only one UI view at a time to the user. In this way, we will avoid confusion created by multiple layers of a UI on top of each other. When the user is using the menu, only MenuCanvas should be visible. When the user is in the game, only inGameCanvas should be visible. Simple!

Let's add a few lines of code to trigger this behavior.

In the GameManager class, add another Canvas type public variable and call it inGameCanvas. We will use this reference to control the enabled state in exactly the same way as we did for menuCanvas. Find the SetGameState function and edit it so that it looks like this:

```
        void SetGameState (GameState newGameState) {

            if (newGameState == GameState.menu) {
                //setup Unity scene for menu state
                menuCanvas.enabled = true;
                inGameCanvas.enabled = false;
            }
            else if (newGameState == GameState.inGame) {
                //setup Unity scene for inGame state
                menuCanvas.enabled = false;
                inGameCanvas.enabled = true;
            }
            else if (newGameState == GameState.gameOver) {
                //setup Unity scene for gameOver state
                menuCanvas.enabled = false;
                inGameCanvas.enabled = false;
            }

            currentGameState = newGameState;
        }
```

Make sure that this time you connect the `inGameCanvas` slot in the inspector to the right game object. Press **Play** in Unity to preview the behavior. If everything works as it should, `MenuCanvas` will disappear as soon as we press the **Play** button and `inGameCanvas` will appear.

Great! It all works fine. The views are switching properly. In the game, the view isn't doing any work at the moment. The score, collected coins, and high score always display zero values. We will take care of this in the next chapter.

I hope it's clear to you how to create additional views for our game. We are missing one more view, `GameOverView`. I would like you to import it and implement it yourself as an exercise. You can find `GameOverView` on the Packt hub. I have named the file `GameOverCanvas.unitypackage`.

Game over

Testing the UI is crucial. To test whether the GameOver view is presented to the user at the right time or not, we need a certain condition to happen. In this case, we are calling game over as soon as the player dies in our game. Let's create the right conditions for this.

At the moment, we are using only one level piece, which is a straight ground level. To make things a bit more interesting and challenging, create a copy of the `LevelPieceBasic` game object and call it `LevelPieceHole`. Delete two sections of the floor and place the `KillCollider` prefab under the hole. Make sure that the `KillCollider` prefab is a child of the `LevelPieceHole` game object.

The last thing to do is add the newly created level piece into `LevelGenerator`. Add `LevelPieceHole` to the **Level Prefabs** list inside `LevelGeneratorComponent`:

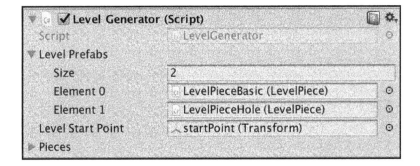

That's it! With these few steps, we have added a new level piece into the game. To test whether the game over canvas is being displayed at the right time or not, let the player fall down the hole.

The code in this chapter

The code for GameManager.cs is as follows:

```
using UnityEngine;
using System.Collections;

public enum GameState {
    menu,
    inGame,
    gameOver
}

public class GameManager : MonoBehaviour {

    public static GameManager instance;
    public GameState currentGameState = GameState.menu;

    public Canvas menuCanvas;
    public Canvas inGameCanvas;
    public Canvas gameOverCanvas;


    void Awake() {
        instance = this;
    }

    void Start() {
        currentGameState = GameState.menu;
    }

    //called to start the game
    public void StartGame() {
        PlayerController.instance.StartGame();
        SetGameState(GameState.inGame);
    }

    //called when player die
    public void GameOver() {
        SetGameState(GameState.gameOver);
    }
```

```
//called when player decide to go back to the menu
public void BackToMenu() {
    SetGameState(GameState.menu);
}

void SetGameState (GameState newGameState) {

    if (newGameState == GameState.menu) {
        //setup Unity scene for menu state
        menuCanvas.enabled = true;
        inGameCanvas.enabled = false;
        gameOverCanvas.enabled = false;
    }
    else if (newGameState == GameState.inGame) {
        //setup Unity scene for inGame state
        menuCanvas.enabled = false;
        inGameCanvas.enabled = true;
        gameOverCanvas.enabled = false;
    }
    else if (newGameState == GameState.gameOver) {
        //setup Unity scene for gameOver state
        menuCanvas.enabled = false;
        inGameCanvas.enabled = false;
        gameOverCanvas.enabled = true;
    }

    currentGameState = newGameState;
}


void Update() {

    if (Input.GetButtonDown("s")) {
        StartGame();
    }
}

}
```

Summary

Well done! You are becoming proficient with using Unity's built-in UI system. In this chapter, you learned about the visual parts of the UI as well as the Event System, which allows interaction with the user. In the next chapter, we will focus on collectibles and storing data between Unity sessions.

13

Collectables

Now that we know how to create the user interface for our game, we can start creating the collectable assets that will be displayed there.

What we will learn here is extremely useful because all the collectables usually share the same foundations, which means that after learning how to create one type of collectable, we also know how to create all the others. In this chapter, we'll start by developing a coin that can be collected by the player, stored in our script and displayed on our UI. We will also take a look how to adapt the same script to work as a different type of collectable and how we can change the gameplay depending on the number of health points or magic points we have.

Collectables

All objects in a game that the player is able to collect are called collectables. In our game, we will add collectable coins scattered in the level's pieces for the player to collect. Before we start working on it, we need to plan what we are going to do, so this is our simple plan:

- Our collectables–let's call them coins from now on–will be collected on contact with the player game object
- We will write the `Collectable` class to manage coin behavior
- For every coin collected, we will count and increment the number of collected coins on the UI
- The count of total collected coins will restart with a new game

The coin prefab

To make things a little easier, we have already prepared the visual part of our coin. Download `Coin.unitypackage` and import it into your project.

Now we drag the **Coin** prefab into the **Hierarchy** view so that we can take a look at it:

To create this coin prefab, we have created an empty `GameObject` and added a **Sprite** `Renderer` to it. In the `Sprite` option we have linked it with the coin sprite, as you can see here:

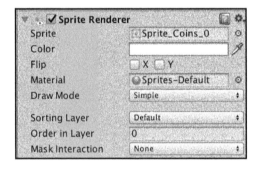

Then we have created a simple animation controlled by the `Animator` with the coin sequence, which gives the sensation that the coin is spinning. To do that, all we need is to open the **Animation** tab (pictured here) that is located under the **Window**:

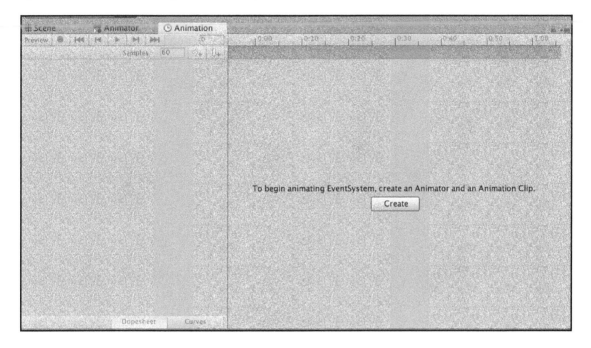

Then we need to click **Create;** it will ask us what name we want to assign to that animation and where we want to save it. After that, we notice that the **Animation** panel now has changed a little bit, this means that we are ready to add some elements to animate:

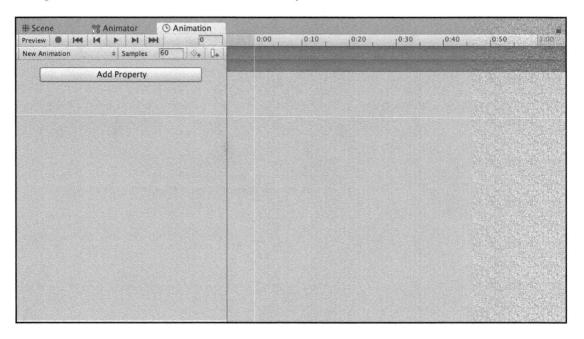

Now all we need to do is drag and drop the sprites that we want to animate one by one, making sure that we put them in order and ideally one sprite per frame, similar to what we have in the coin prefab:

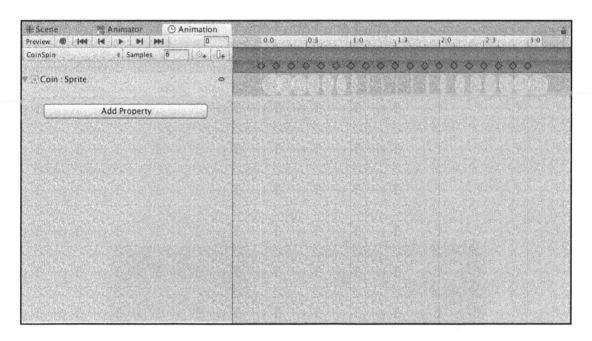

Now that we know how to create a simple 2D animation inside Unity, let's continue with the coin prefab.

Most collectables react with the environment through the physics of the game. We can use the 2D trigger here to react with the `Player` Game Object's `Rigidbody2D` component. This is exactly the same way we inserted `LeaveTriggers` into the game previously.

Select the coin and add the `CircleCollider2D` component. A green circle will appear around the coin, representing the triggering area. Make sure you tweak the radius value to roughly match the size of the coin. In my case, a value of 0.35 works great.

Another requirement that we need to fulfill to make the trigger work is ticking the `IsTrigger` checkbox, and our coin is ready to process trigger events. All that we need to do now is write some code to manage its behavior.

The Collectable class

Let's plan what behavior we want from our collectable. We will need the following methods:

- Show(): This will show the coin and activate its collider
- Hide(): This will hide the coin and deactivate its collider
- Collect(): This is called at the moment of collection of the coin
- OnTriggerEnter2D(Collider2D other): This is called by Unity's physics system when the collider enters our coin's trigger

Create a new C# script, call it Collectable, and write the following code:

```csharp
using UnityEngine;
using System.Collections;

public class Collectable : MonoBehaviour {

    bool isCollected = false;

    void Show() {
        this.GetComponent<SpriteRenderer>().enabled = true;
        this.GetComponent<CircleCollider2D>().enabled = true;
        isCollected = false;
    }

    void Hide() {
        this.GetComponent<SpriteRenderer>().enabled = false;
        this.GetComponent<CircleCollider2D>().enabled = false;
    }


    void Collect() {

        isCollected = true;
        Hide();

    }

    void OnTriggerEnter2D(Collider2D other) {

        if (other.tag == "Player") {
            Collect();
        }
    }
}
```

Add the Collectable script to your coin prefab. We are ready to test it now! Make the coin prefab a child of one of the level chunks. Create a few copies of the coin next to each other so that you can test them better.

Let's click **Play** in Unity and see what happens. You should notice that the coin disappears upon contact with the `Player` game object. That's exactly what we wanted.

The last thing to do now is count the collected coins. We will store the number of coins collected in the `GameManager` class and increment the `int` number every time a coin is collected. Let's add some functionality to the `GameManager` class:

1. Add the `collectedCoins` public member:

   ```
   public int collectedCoins = 0;
   ```

2. Add a `public` method that you can call when a coin is collected:

   ```
   public void CollectedCoin() {
      collectedCoins ++;
   }
   ```

   What this method does is increment the `collectedCoins` variable by 1 every time the ++ operator is used.

3. In the `Collectable` class, add a single line calling `CollectedCoin()` from the `Collect` method, as follows:

   ```
   void Collect() {

       isCollected = true;
       Hide();
       GameManager.instance.CollectedCoin();
   }
   ```

Now click **Play** in Unity. Let's take a quick look to check whether it works. Select **GameManager** and press the **Play** button. You will notice that the number of collected coins in the Unity **Inspector** increases every time a new coin is collected. Great! We now know that our `collectedCoin` variable works. However, we still need to update the label value in the `gameView` so that our user can see exactly how many coins they have collected.

It's a good idea to keep UI–controlling code separate from the `GameManager`. Let's write a short script that controls the UI in the **Game View**. Create and add this component to the `InGameCanvas` game object:

```
using UnityEngine;
using UnityEngine.UI;
using System.Collections;

public class ViewInGame : MonoBehaviour {

    public Text coinLabel;

    void Update() {
        if (GameManager.instance.currentGameState == GameState.inGame) {
            coinLabel.text = GameManager.instance.collectedCoins.ToString();
        }
    }
}
```

Once you have the **View In Game** component added, drag the `coinLabel` game object into the **coinsLabel** slot:

The **View In Game** component should look like this:

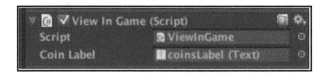

What our code does is update the `.text` string value on the label. By doing this, the text on the UI changes and is always up-to-date with the `collectedCoins` value in **Game Manager**.

High score and persisting data

Pretty much every game has some sort of scoring system. You will now learn how to write simple code that calculates the score based on the distance the player has traveled since the start of the level. We will then use this score value and store it in Unity's `PlayerPrefs` class to make sure that the value is remembered between sessions. `PlayerPrefs` is a very useful built–in Unity class that allows us to store and access data between Unity sessions.

Let's write the following method in the `Player` class:

```
public float GetDistance() {

    float traveledDistance = Vector2.Distance(new Vector2(startingPosition.x, 0),
                                              new Vector2(this.transform.position.x, 0));
    return traveledDistance;
}
```

We have finally come to a real–life example of a method that returns something. As you can see, the `GetDistance()` method returns a float value, the distance between the starting point and the current position of the player game object.

I won't go into too much detail here. I encourage you to dive into the Unity **Scripting Reference** and search for `Vector2.Distance` to understand exactly how it works.

With the `GetDistance()` method working, we can now call it from any place in the code and get the accurate distance traveled by the `Player` game object. The value returned by this method will be used directly as the player's score. Now is a good time to connect the score UI label directly to the `GetDistance()` method.

In the `ViewInGame` class, we declare the `scoreLabel` `Text` variable and add a new line to the `Update()` method just before the line where we are assigning the coin label:

```
1   using UnityEngine;
2   using UnityEngine.UI;
3   using System.Collections;
4
5   public class ViewInGame : MonoBehaviour {
6
7       public Text scoreLabel;
8       public Text coinLabel;
9
10      void Update() {
11          if (GameManager.instance.currentGameState == GameState.inGame) {
12              scoreLabel.text = PlayerController.instance.GetDistance().ToString("f0");
13              coinLabel.text = GameManager.instance.collectedCoins.ToString();
14          }
15      }
16  }
```

Notice line **12**. We are assigning the `scoreLabel.text` value by taking it directly from the float value returned from the `PlayerController.instance.GetDistance()` method. I hope this is not confusing! If it is, please remember what we said in the very early chapters of this book: a function can be the substitute for a value. In this case, when we call `GetInstance()`, we get an `int` number back straightaway. All we need to do is convert that float into a string. To do this, we use the `ToString()` function right away.

You are probably wondering, "What is the magical `f0` parameter that we are passing in `ToString("f0")`?" It describes how we want our string to be formatted. In this case, we just want a whole number, without any decimals. I encourage you to read more online about C# `ToString()` formatting.

The last thing to do is connect the `scoreLabel` variable with the actual `scoreLabel` game object in the **Hierarchy** view. When you are ready, click **Play** in Unity. The score label in the top–left corner will be showing the correct score value. Great job!

What you just learned is how to convert a float value to a string and display the value in the UI for the user.

We are getting close to finishing writing the functionality for the `inGameView`. We will now work on persisting data. What does this mean? We want the user's high score to be remembered between game sessions. So, if the user closes the game and then opens it again, their high score will not be reset to zero. Rather, the game will remember their best score.

Unity does have an easy–to–use system for this. Let's jump into the scripting reference and search for `PlayerPrefs`.

Let's take a look at the list of static functions again, specifically at the `SetFloat` and `GetFloat` functions:

- `SetFloat(string key, float value)`: This sets the value of the preference identified by the key.
- `public static float GetFloat(string key, float defaultValue = 0.0F)`: This returns the value corresponding to the key in the preference file if it exists. If it doesn't exist, it will return `defaultValue`.

In other words, we can ask Unity to save the float value accessible under the string key. Let's jump straight into our code. Open the `PlayerController` script and add the high–score–saving code.

```
71   public void Kill() {
72
73       GameManager.instance.GameOver();
74       animator.SetBool("isAlive", false);
75
76       //check if highscore save if it is
77       if (PlayerPrefs.GetFloat("highscore", 0) < this.GetDistance()) {
78           //save new highscore
79           PlayerPrefs.SetFloat("highscore", this.GetDistance());
80       }
81   }
```

What are we doing here? At the moment when the player is killed, we check whether the current distance traveled is greater than the float value stored under the high score key in `PlayerPrefs`. If the distance is greater, it means the user has achieved a new high score, so Unity proceeds to line **79** and overrides the value in `PlayerPrefs`. Saving done!

Now, we need to make sure that `highscoreLabel` is displaying the correct value all the time. Add a new `Text` type variable, call it `highscoreLabel` this time, and add a line to the `Update` function.

 Make sure that all public member slots are connected to the correct game objects to avoid *Null Reference Exceptions*.

Our high score should work now. Play a game. Let the character die, restart the game, and see whether the value is displayed in the top–right corner.

Health Points and Health bar

Now that we have successfully created a collectable coin and developed a counting system for it, we can take a look at other types of collectables that are commonly used in video games.

The first one is the **Health Point**; it is very common to see this type of collectable in multiple game genres and it allows us to have a health system–that way, we can get hit a few times before dying.

Let's start by downloading `Health.unitypackage` and importing it into your project. Now drag the **Health** prefab into the **Hierarchy** view so that we can take a look at it. If we press **Play**, we can see that it is a simple heart sprite that bounces up and down.

At this moment, nothing will happen if the character touches the heart, so the next thing that we need to do is code our **Health** prefab. Collectables generally have the same principles; they need to be collected, and if we think about it, Health Points behave just like the **Coins**. For that reason, we can start by duplicating the Collectable script and rename it `HealthPoint`. Remember to change the name in the public class (see the following image); otherwise it won't work and it will give an error when you try to play the game:

```
1 using UnityEngine;
2 using System.Collections;

public class HealthPoint : MonoBehaviour {

6     bool isCollected = false;
7
8     void Show() {
```

In this script, we are going to update some lines of code that tell the player it has collected a health point:

```
20    void Collect() {
21
22        isCollected = true;
23        Hide();
24        PlayerController.instance.CollectedHealth();
25    }
```

Instead of connecting this script to the `GameManager`, like we had with the **Coin**, we connect it directly to the `PlayerController`. Now we need to open the `PlayerController` script, and on the variables part we are going to create a new variable called `healthPoints`:

```
4 public class PlayerController : MonoBehaviour {
5
6     public static PlayerController instance;
7
8     public float jumpForce = 6f;
9     public float runningSpeed = 1.5f;
10    public Animator animator;
11
12    private Vector3 startingPosition;
13    private Rigidbody2D rigidBody;
14
15    private int healthPoints;
16
```

Then write the following code just before the last bracket:

```
86    public void CollectedHealth() {
87        healthPoints ++;
88    }
```

As we can see, the principles that we have used to create a collectable coin are very similar to the **Health Point**, but instead of assigning it to the `GameManager`, we have assigned it to the `PlayerController`.

Now that our character knows when he collects a Health Point, in the next chapter, we will define how many points he starts the game with and give him a few enemies or obstacles that can take those **Health Points** away.

Magic Points and Magic bar

Magic Points has a different purpose than **Coins** or **Health Points**, usually, we use it to fire some powers, to do a special move, or any other cool thing that we might think of. It has a vivid purpose to collect them because it will change the gameplay, so at this point, we may assume that the way we create it is totally different–but actually no. As we saw previously, the way we collect objects in terms of functionality is the same, a character touches the collectable and receives the information that they have done that. Then we can choose what we want to do with that information, do we simply sum the number of objects that we collected to be used as a score, or will the object give the character some benefits such as more health or magic points.

When we think this way, we start to realize that our possibilities are now endless and we are able to create many things just by understanding the principles. Let's see how we could create a simple **Magic Bar** or **Energy Bar** that allows our character to jump higher, for example.

The first thing we do is duplicate the **Collectable** script, rename the file to **MagicPoint**, and then we change the `Collect()` part:

```
20    void Collect() {
21
22        isCollected = true;
23        Hide();
24        PlayerController.instance.CollectedMagic();
25    }
```

This sends the information to the character that they have collected a **Magic Point**. Now, inside `PlayerController` we add an `int` variable with the name `magicPoints` and we add this `void CollectedMagic()` that sums the magic points:

```
87    public void CollectedMagic() {
88        magicPoints ++;
89    }
```

Once we have this structure created, all we need to do is define what is possible to do with a certain amount of **Magic Points**. Let's tell the character that he can jump higher if he has more than 5 **Magic Points**.

To do that, we simply update the `Jump` function, saying that if the player presses the jump button and the character has less than 5 Magic Points, the jump will be normal, but if the player presses the jump button and the character has more than 5 Magic Points, the jump will be two times higher than normal, (`jumpForce*2`):

```
50    void Jump() {
51        if (isGrounded() && magicPoints < 5) {
52            rigidBody.AddForce(Vector2.up * jumpForce, ForceMode2D.Impulse);
53        }
54
55        if (isGrounded() && magicPoints > 5) {
56            rigidBody.AddForce(Vector2.up * (jumpForce * 2), ForceMode2D.Impulse);
57        }
58    }
```

That's it, we have created a simple and functional system with **Magic Points**, now if we want, we can define unique abilities that only happen when our character has a certain amount of **Magic Points**. This is a great opportunity to explore what we have learned so far by trying to develop an ability all by yourself, personalizing the game to your taste.

The code in this chapter

Let's take a look at the code again to make sure we are on the same page.

The code for `Collectable.cs` is as follows:

```
using UnityEngine;
using System.Collections;

public class Collectable : MonoBehaviour {
    bool isCollected = false;
```

```
  void Show() {
    this.GetComponent<SpriteRenderer>().enabled = true;
    this.GetComponent<CircleCollider2D>().enabled = true;
    isCollected = false;
  }

  void Hide() {
    this.GetComponent<SpriteRenderer>().enabled = false;
    this.GetComponent<CircleCollider2D>().enabled = false;
  }


  void Collect() {

    isCollected = true;
    Hide();
    GameManager.instance.CollectedCoin();
  }

  void OnTriggerEnter2D(Collider2D other) {
    if (other.tag == "Player") {
      Collect();
    }
  }
}
}
```

Here is the code for HealthPoint:

```
using UnityEngine;
using System.Collections;

public class HealthPoint : MonoBehaviour {

    bool isCollected = false;

    void Show() {
        this.GetComponent<SpriteRenderer>().enabled = true;
        this.GetComponent<CircleCollider2D>().enabled = true;
        isCollected = false;
    }

    void Hide() {
        this.GetComponent<SpriteRenderer>().enabled = false;
        this.GetComponent<CircleCollider2D>().enabled = false;
    }


    void Collect() {
```

```
            isCollected = true;
            Hide();
            PlayerController.instance.CollectedHealth();
        }

    void OnTriggerEnter2D(Collider2D other) {

            if (other.tag == "Player") {
                Collect();
            }
        }
    }
}
```

The following is the code for `MagicPoint`:

```
using UnityEngine;
using System.Collections;

public class MagicPoint : MonoBehaviour {

    bool isCollected = false;

    void Show() {
        this.GetComponent<SpriteRenderer>().enabled = true;
        this.GetComponent<CircleCollider2D>().enabled = true;
        isCollected = false;
    }

    void Hide() {
        this.GetComponent<SpriteRenderer>().enabled = false;
        this.GetComponent<CircleCollider2D>().enabled = false;
    }


    void Collect() {

        isCollected = true;
        Hide();
        PlayerController.instance.CollectedMagic();
    }

    void OnTriggerEnter2D(Collider2D other) {

        if (other.tag == "Player") {
            Collect();
        }
    }
}
```

This is the code for `playerController.cs`:

```
using UnityEngine;
using System.Collections;

public class PlayerController : MonoBehaviour {

  public static PlayerController instance;

  public float jumpForce = 6f;
  public float runningSpeed = 1.5f;
  public Animator animator;

  private Vector3 startingPosition;
  private Rigidbody2D rigidBody;

  private int healthPoints;
  private int magicPoints;

  void Awake() {
    instance = this;
    rigidBody = GetComponent<Rigidbody2D>();
    startingPosition = this.transform.position;
  }
  public void StartGame() {
    animator.SetBool("isAlive", true);
    this.transform.position = startingPosition;
  }
  void Update () {

    if (GameManager.instance.currentGameState == GameState.inGame)
    {
      if (Input.GetMouseButtonDown(0)) {
        Jump();
      }
      animator.SetBool("isGrounded", isGrounded());
    }
  }

  void FixedUpdate() {

    if (GameManager.instance.currentGameState == GameState.inGame)
    {
      if (rigidBody.velocity.x < runningSpeed) {
        rigidBody.velocity = new Vector2(runningSpeed,
rigidBody.velocity.y);
      }
```

```csharp
    }
  }

  void Jump() {
    if (isGrounded() && magicPoints < 5) {
      rigidBody.AddForce(Vector2.up * jumpForce, ForceMode2D.Impulse);
    }

    if (isGrounded() && magicPoints > 5){
      rigidBody.AddForce(Vector2.up * (jumpForce * 2),
ForceMode2D.Impulse);
    }
  }

  public LayerMask groundLayer;

  bool isGrounded() {

    if (Physics2D.Raycast(this.transform.position, Vector2.down, 0.2f,
groundLayer.value)) {
      return true;
    }
    else {
      return false;
    }
  }

  public void Kill() {
    GameManager.instance.GameOver();
    animator.SetBool("isAlive", false);

    //check if highscore save if it is
    if (PlayerPrefs.GetFloat("highscore", 0) < this.GetDistance()) {
      //save new highscore
      PlayerPrefs.SetFloat("highscore", this.GetDistance());
    }
  }


  public float GetDistance() {
    float traveledDistance = Vector2.Distance(new
Vector2(startingPosition.x, 0),
                                             new
Vector2(this.transform.position.x, 0));
    return traveledDistance;
  }

  public void CollectedHealth() {
```

```
      healthPoints ++;
  }

  public void CollectedMagic(){
     magicPoints ++;
  }


  }
```

The code for ViewInGame.cs is as follows:

```
using UnityEngine;
using UnityEngine.UI;
using System.Collections;

public class ViewInGame : MonoBehaviour {

  public Text scoreLabel;
  public Text coinLabel;
  public Text highscoreLabel;


  void Update() {
     if (GameManager.instance.currentGameState == GameState.inGame) {
        scoreLabel.text =
PlayerController.instance.GetDistance().ToString("f0");
        coinLabel.text = GameManager.instance.collectedCoins.ToString();
        highscoreLabel.text = PlayerPrefs.GetFloat("highscore",
0).ToString("f0");
     }
  }
}
The code for GameManager.cs:
using UnityEngine;
using System.Collections;

public enum GameState {
  menu,
  inGame,
  gameOver
}

public class GameManager : MonoBehaviour {

  public static GameManager instance;
  public GameState currentGameState = GameState.menu;
```

```
public Canvas menuCanvas;
public Canvas inGameCanvas;
public Canvas gameOverCanvas;

public int collectedCoins = 0;

void Awake() {
  instance = this;
}

void Start() {
  currentGameState = GameState.menu;
}
//called to start the game
public void StartGame() {
  PlayerController.instance.StartGame();
  SetGameState(GameState.inGame);
}
//called when player die
public void GameOver() {
  SetGameState(GameState.gameOver);
}

//called when player decide to go back to the menu
public void BackToMenu() {
  SetGameState(GameState.menu);
}

void SetGameState (GameState newGameState) {
  if (newGameState == GameState.menu) {
    //setup Unity scene for menu state
    menuCanvas.enabled = true;
    inGameCanvas.enabled = false;
    gameOverCanvas.enabled = false;
  }
  else if (newGameState == GameState.inGame) {
    //setup Unity scene for inGame state
    menuCanvas.enabled = false;
    inGameCanvas.enabled = true;
    gameOverCanvas.enabled = false;
  }
  else if (newGameState == GameState.gameOver) {
    //setup Unity scene for gameOver state
    menuCanvas.enabled = false;
    inGameCanvas.enabled = false;
    gameOverCanvas.enabled = true;
  }
  currentGameState = newGameState;
```

```
    }


    void Update() {

      if (Input.GetButtonDown("s")) {
        StartGame();
      }
    }


    public void CollectedCoin() {
      collectedCoins ++;
    }

  }
```

Summary

In this chapter, you learned about collectables, counting the player's score, and persisting data.

On the next chapter, we will take a look at how to create simple enemies, making our game more challenging and allowing us to add a greater variety of obstacles. We will learn how to make the enemy move and attack.

14
Enemies

Step by step we have learned the foundations of how to create a game from scratch and, at this point, we are able to think of a simple game design and execute it. We know how to develop the main character, the level, the winning and losing conditions, collectibles, and a few more things, but one topic is missing: the enemies.

In this chapter, we will take a look at how to create some basic enemies so we can implement them in our games.

What makes an enemy?

In a video game, anything can be an obstacle and anything can be an enemy; it can start out as something harmless and suddenly become a threat, it can move from side to side or stay in the same position all the time, it can be predictable or not, and so on. The main focus here will be to learn the basic functionalities of an enemy and then we can choose whether we want to use them or not; that way we can create different type of enemies, just by choosing what we allow them to do.

As we can see in the following image, using this method, we are able to create a few distinct enemies:

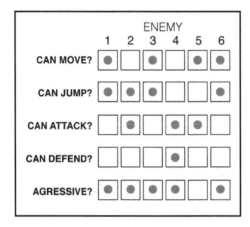

This is a great approach, especially at the stage where we are still creating our first game; we can add a little bit of variety to our enemies and all of them share the same script.

Movement

The first thing on our list that we have chosen to work on is the movement. The lesson that we'll cover on this topic can be used both on enemies and on movable obstacles, so it's very useful.

There are a few ways to make enemies move and, probably like the rest of the lessons that we have learned so far, we'll eventually adapt and find our own way of creating things, so it adjusts perfectly with what we want. In this chapter, we'll take a look at three ways to make the enemies move.

Movement by animation

This is probably the simplest approach to make a character or obstacle move, although it's still very useful and practical if we don't need a complex movement system.

In the previous chapter, we created a sprite animation for the coin where we added a different sprite for each frame of the animation and, at the end, we saw the coin spinning. Well, here we'll be using the same animation tab, where it contains a timeline, but the way we create the animation will be completely different:

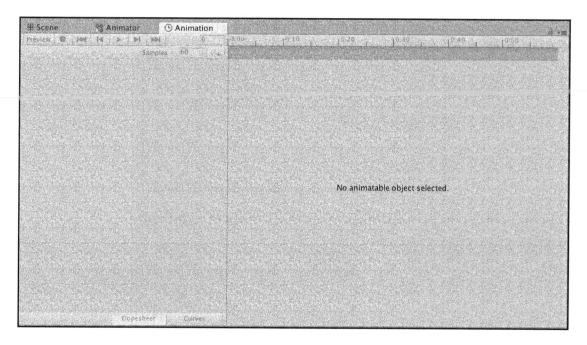

Let's start by selecting the object that we want to animate. For this example, we have chosen a piece of the floor sprite, to create a moveable platform, but remember this can also be applied to an enemy character. To do this, let's create an empty GameObject, name it **Platform**, and then simply drag and drop the **Floor** prefab inside the GameObject that we just created. It should look like this:

If we want the platform to be bigger or smaller, this is the perfect time to change it. Then, select the **Platform** GameObject (not the **Floor** prefab), open the **Animation** tab, and click the button that says **Create**:

It will ask you the name and where you want to save the animation. Place it inside the animations folder and name it Platform:

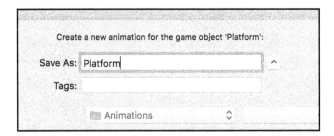

Now we need to click the **Add Property** button > **Transform** > **Position**:

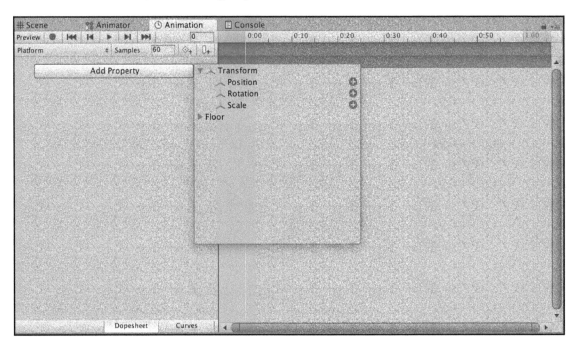

What does this do? It allows us to animate the **Transform** position of the **object** or **character** that we want to animate and that is exactly what we need to do in order to make our platform move from side to side.

Let's click the red circle that represents the record button:

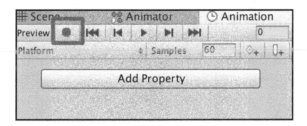

We need to click this button before we start animating; doing this will start recording all the changes that we make on the object.

Put the **Animation** window in a different tab than the **Scene** window–that way we can animate directly on the **Scene** window and see the changes being made on the **Animation** timeline.

On the timeline, go to the 1:00 second, where we already have an automatic keyframe created:

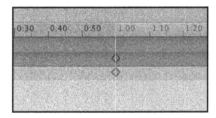

Then click the Platform and move it a little bit to the right:

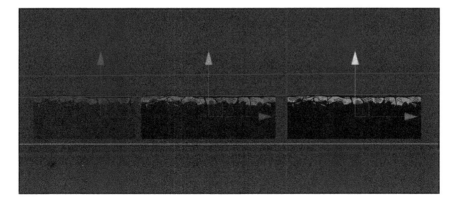

Now let's click the **Record** button again and test the animation that we have just created by clicking the **Play** button. As we can see, we already have an object that moves from left to right. Before using this platform, we need to make it loop so the animation looks seamless. To do this, we simply need to copy the first frame and paste on the 2:00 second, that way it will go from left to right and then from right to left again.

Select the first frame, copy it by using *Ctrl + C* or *Command + C* (we cannot do it with the right mouse click), move to the frame on the 2:00 second, and paste it with *Ctrl + V* or *Command + V*, it should look like this:

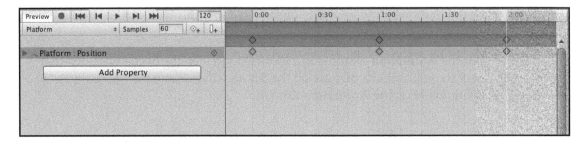

That's it, we have a perfect animation loop created and our platform is ready to be used. Save it as a prefab by dragging and dropping `Platform GameObject` into the prefab folder.

Once that's done, we can create new `LevelPieces` and add the `Platform` prefab onto them.

Trigger movement

Another type of movement that we can implement on our enemies or platforms is the trigger movement. This is also a basic way to create movement, where the enemy or platform is moving in one direction until it collides against something and then returns back. We can see this on multiple games, especially 2D platforms.

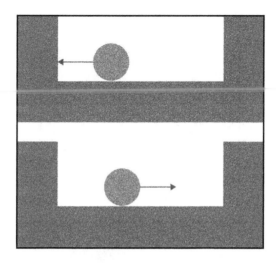

As we can see in the preceding image, the green circle represents the enemy and the red arrow represents the trigger distance. When the trigger touches the wall, the enemy turns around and moves in the opposite direction.

When should we use this method instead of the animation one? Using the animation movement, we are setting the distance limit, the enemy or platform won't move differently no matter where it is placed. On the other hand, by using the trigger method, the distance traveled is dynamic.

This example doesn't necessarily fit into our game, as we don't have any walls yet, but it is still relevant to explain how to do it, so we have to know how to implement it in the future. The simple way to do this is by creating an empty object, name it `TriggerMovement`, for example, and drag and drop it inside the enemy/platform:

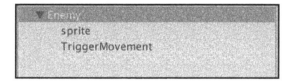

Then we make sure that the transform position of the `TriggerMovement` is set to zero:

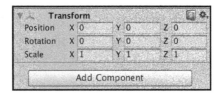

Now we add a new Box Collider 2D component to the `TriggerMovement`. We have to place the `TriggerMovement` object in front of our enemy, we should place it within the distance that we want the enemy to turn around when the trigger touches something:

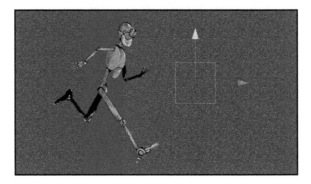

For example, if this was the evil twin of our main character and we made it an enemy of the game, we would place the `TriggerMovement` object slightly in front of the character. This way, the character itself doesn't need to necessarily touch the wall before turning around.

Then we could simply add a script to our `TriggerMovement` object that informs the character that he is near a wall, so he can turn around and move in the opposite direction until he hits another wall again.

To create this enemy, we have used `PlayerController` as a template script, then we changed a few things so that the player can't control this character:

```
1  using System.Collections;
2  using System.Collections.Generic;
3  using UnityEngine;
4
5  public class Enemy : MonoBehaviour {
6
7      public float jumpForce = 6f;
8      public float runningSpeed = 1.5f;
9      public Animator animator;
10
11     private Rigidbody2D rigidBody;
12
13     public static bool turnAround;
14
15     void Awake() {
16         rigidBody = GetComponent<Rigidbody2D>();
17     }
18
19     public void StartGame() {
20         animator.SetBool("isAlive", true);
21     }
22
23
24     void FixedUpdate() {
25
26         if (GameManager.instance.currentGameState == GameState.inGame)
27         {
28             if (rigidBody.velocity.x < runningSpeed) {
29                 rigidBody.velocity = new Vector2(runningSpeed, rigidBody.velocity.y);
30             }
31         }
32     }
33
34     void Jump() {
35         if (isGrounded()) {
36             rigidBody.AddForce(Vector2.up * jumpForce, ForceMode2D.Impulse);
37         }
38     }
39
40     public LayerMask groundLayer;
41
42     bool isGrounded() {
43
44         if (Physics2D.Raycast(this.transform.position, Vector2.down, 0.2f, groundLayer.value)) {
45             return true;
46         }
47         else {
48             return false;
49         }
50     }
51
52
53     public void Kill() {
54         animator.SetBool("isAlive", false);
55     }
56
57 }
58
```

So with this script, our character will simply run forward all the time. To make it turn around and run in the opposite direction, we need to link `TriggerMovement` with this character. We can see on line **13** that we have already created a public static bool with the name `turnAround`. This will allow scripts that are assigned to other objects to send information into this script.

Now let's create a new script that will be added to the `TriggerMovement` object. We can name it `triggerMovement`, that way we know that this script belongs to the `TriggerMovement` object:

```
1  using System.Collections;
2  using System.Collections.Generic;
3  using UnityEngine;
4
5  public class triggerMovement : MonoBehaviour {
6
7      public bool movingForward;
8
9      void OnTriggerEnter(Collider other) {
10
11         if (movingForward == true)
12         {
13             Enemy.turnAround = true;
14         }
15
16         else
17         {
18             Enemy.turnAround = false;
19         }
20
21     }
22 }
23
```

And this is all we need to write inside the `triggerMovement` script. It checks whether the object has collided against anything and if it has, it gives the information to the enemy to turn around. If it is moving forward, it will turn around and move backward, if it is moving backward, it will turn around and move forward.

Now, all we need to do is to open the Enemy script and use this information to make the character change the move direction:

```
1  using System.Collections;
2  using System.Collections.Generic;
3  using UnityEngine;
4
5  public class Enemy : MonoBehaviour {
6
7      public float jumpForce = 6f;
8      public float runningSpeed = 1.5f;
9      public Animator animator;
10
11     private Rigidbody2D rigidBody;
12
13     public static bool turnAround;
14
15     void Awake() {
16         rigidBody = GetComponent<Rigidbody2D>();
17     }
18
19     void Start(){
20         turnAround = false;
21     }
22
23     public void StartGame() {
24         animator.SetBool("isAlive", true);
25     }
26
27
28     void FixedUpdate() {
29
30         if (turnAround == true)
31         {
32             transform.eulerAngles = new Vector3(0,180,0);
33         }
34
35         if (turnAround == false)
36         {
37             transform.eulerAngles = new Vector3(0,0,0);
38         }
39
40         if (GameManager.instance.currentGameState == GameState.inGame)
41         {
42             if (rigidBody.velocity.x < runningSpeed) {
43                 rigidBody.velocity = new Vector2(runningSpeed, rigidBody.velocity.y);
44             }
45         }
46     }
47
```

As we can see on line **19**, we define that at the start of the game, the character, by default, should move forward, so the turnAround bool is set to false. This is necessary when dealing with static variables because even if we restart the game, the script will remember the last value and if we don't state the value that we want at the start of the script, the value assigned will be the last one.

Then starting on line **30** to line **38**, we explain what happens to the character when the turnAround variable is set to true or false. In this case, the character will flip to the other direction, soon the triggerMovement gives the information that it has touched something.

To achieve the flip effect, we have used the `transform.eulerAngles`. For example, when the `turnAround` variable is set to true, the character uses `transform.eulerAngles` to set the *y* rotation axis to 180 degrees, which means that we'll be facing the opposite direction and when we set that value to 0 degrees, it will face forward.

Making it an enemy

Now that we have the enemy moving inside our game, we need to set it as an Enemy, so the player dies when touching him. This is fairly simple to do, all we need is to create a new tag for the `Enemy` prefab and call it **Enemy** as well. To do this, click **Tag** and then click **Add Tag:**

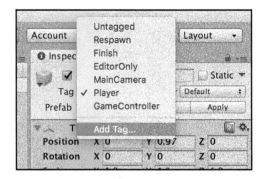

Then click the **plus** sign:

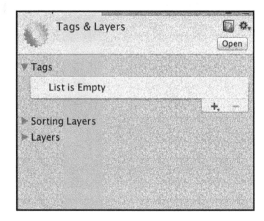

Name the Tag as `Enemy`, save the prefab, and that's it. Now let's open the `PlayerController` script and add this line of code:

```
64
65      void OnCollisionEnter(Collision other) {
66
67          if (other.gameObject.tag == "Enemy") {
68              Kill ();
69          }
70      }
71
72
```

That's it; now if our character touches an enemy, it will die.

The code in this chapter

The code for `Enemy.cs`:

```
using System.Collections;
using System.Collections.Generic;
using UnityEngine;

public class Enemy : MonoBehaviour {

    public float jumpForce = 6f;
    public float runningSpeed = 1.5f;
    public Animator animator;

    private Rigidbody2D rigidBody;

    public static bool turnAround;

    void Awake() {
        rigidBody = GetComponent<Rigidbody2D>();
    }

    void Start(){
        turnAround = false;
    }

    public void StartGame() {
        animator.SetBool("isAlive", true);
    }
```

```
    void FixedUpdate() {

        if (turnAround == true)
        {
            transform.eulerAngles = new Vector3(0,180,0);
        }

        if (turnAround == false)
        {
            transform.eulerAngles = new Vector3(0,0,0);
        }

        if (GameManager.instance.currentGameState == GameState.inGame)
        {
            if (rigidBody.velocity.x < runningSpeed) {
                rigidBody.velocity = new Vector2(runningSpeed,
rigidBody.velocity.y);
            }
        }
    }

    void Jump() {
        if (isGrounded()) {
            rigidBody.AddForce(Vector2.up * jumpForce,
ForceMode2D.Impulse);
        }
    }

    public LayerMask groundLayer;

    bool isGrounded() {

        if (Physics2D.Raycast(this.transform.position, Vector2.down, 0.2f,
groundLayer.value)) {
            return true;
        }
        else {
            return false;
        }
    }


    public void Kill() {
        animator.SetBool("isAlive", false);
    }

}
```

The code for `triggerMovement.cs`:

```
using System.Collections;
using System.Collections.Generic;
using UnityEngine;

public class triggerMovement : MonoBehaviour {

    public bool movingForward;

    void OnTriggerEnter(Collider other) {

        if (movingForward == true)
        {
            Enemy.turnAround = true;
        }

        else
        {
            Enemy.turnAround = false;
        }

    }
}
```

The code for `PlayerController.cs`:

```
using UnityEngine;
using System.Collections;

public class PlayerController : MonoBehaviour {

    public static PlayerController instance;

    public float jumpForce = 6f;
    public float runningSpeed = 1.5f;
    public Animator animator;

    private Vector3 startingPosition;
    private Rigidbody2D rigidBody;

    void Awake() {
        instance = this;
        rigidBody = GetComponent<Rigidbody2D>();
        startingPosition = this.transform.position;
    }

    public void StartGame() {
```

```
            animator.SetBool("isAlive", true);
            this.transform.position = startingPosition;
    }

    void Update () {

        if (GameManager.instance.currentGameState == GameState.inGame)
        {
            if (Input.GetMouseButtonDown(0)) {
                Jump();
            }
            animator.SetBool("isGrounded", isGrounded());
        }
    }

    void FixedUpdate() {

        if (GameManager.instance.currentGameState == GameState.inGame)
        {
            if (rigidBody.velocity.x < runningSpeed) {
                rigidBody.velocity = new Vector2(runningSpeed,
rigidBody.velocity.y);
            }
        }
    }

    void Jump() {
        if (isGrounded()) {
            rigidBody.AddForce(Vector2.up * jumpForce,
ForceMode2D.Impulse);
        }
    }

    public LayerMask groundLayer;

    bool isGrounded() {

        if (Physics2D.Raycast(this.transform.position, Vector2.down, 0.2f,
groundLayer.value)) {
            return true;
        }
        else {
            return false;
        }
    }

    void OnCollisionEnter(Collision other) {
```

```
        if (other.gameObject.tag == "Enemy") {
            Kill ();
        }
    }


    public void Kill() {
        GameManager.instance.GameOver();
        animator.SetBool("isAlive", false);

        //check if highscore save if it is
        if (PlayerPrefs.GetFloat("highscore", 0) < this.GetDistance()) {
            //save new highscore
            PlayerPrefs.SetFloat("highscore", this.GetDistance());
        }
    }


    public float GetDistance() {
        float traveledDistance = Vector2.Distance(new
Vector2(startingPosition.x, 0),
                                                  new
Vector2(this.transform.position.x, 0));
        return traveledDistance;
    }


}
```

Summary

In this chapter, we have learned how to create a simple enemy, the different ways of making them move, and how to set the character as an enemy, where the player needs to avoid touching them or it will die.

In the next chapter, we will take a look on how to optimize, export, and the fundamentals of how to create a 3D game based on what we have learned so far.

15
Audio, 3D Games, and Export

We are now entering the final chapter of the book, and at this point, we can call ourselves game designers because we now know how to make games from scratch using C#. But there are still a few things that are important to know and we will address them in this chapter. We'll take a look at how to properly export the game to different platforms, what we need to know to create a 3D game, how to add music, how to add sound, how to optimize the game, and a few interesting tips that will help us create amazing games.

How to add sound effects and music

A game isn't complete without sound or, it makes the experience much more enjoyable and helps to transmit emotions. So let's take a look at how we can add music and sounds to our projects and how we can use them.

Where to find sound effects and music

The first thing that we need is to have the audio files. Unless we know how to make music, we need to search for them online, so we have prepared a small list with useful links where you can legally download audio files to use on your games:

Royalty Free :

- www.incompetech.com
- www.bensound.com
- www.freesound.org
- www.freesfx.co.uk
- www.zapsplat.com

- www.soundbible.com
- www.audiomicro.com
- www.soundeffectsplus.com

Premium :

- www.pond5.com
- www.audioblocks.com
- www.premiumbeat.com
- www.audiohero.com
- www.audiojungle.net
- www.tunefruit.com

With this list, we should be able to find any sound effect or music that we need for our game, even on the free websites we have plenty of variety, so don't get discouraged if you plan on creating a game with no budget.

Adding music

For this example, we have chosen music and a sound effect to add to the game that we have been developing. Using the previously mentioned websites, try to search for a sound effect for the jump and music that would go well with the game. Then, create a folder, name it **Audio** (to do this, just right–click an empty space on the **Assets** panel and go to **Create | Folder**), and inside that folder import the two audio files that you have downloaded, it should look like this:

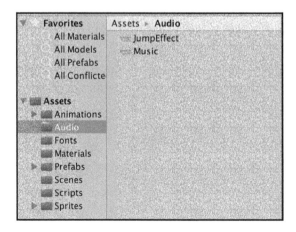

Now we are going to create an **empty** GameObject:

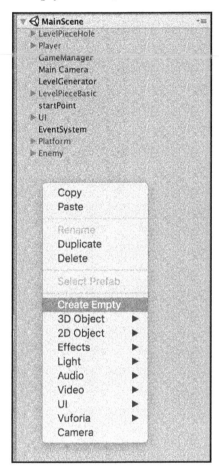

This `GameObject` will be responsible for the game music, so let's name it `BackgroundMusic`. The next step will be to add an `Audio Source` component. To do this, select the `BackgroundMusic` object and click **Add Component**. Select **Audio** and then **Audio Source:**

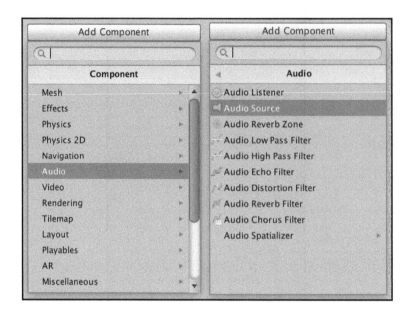

Now on it says **AudioClip**, we are going to click the little circle with a dot inside, this will open a window so we can choose the audio file that we want to use:

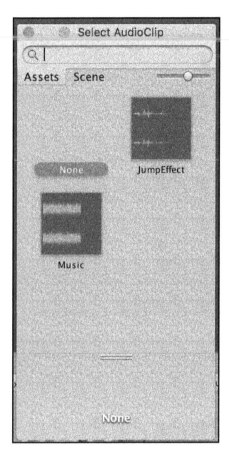

Double–click the audio file that you want. Now let's make sure that the music plays throughout the entire game and that it doesn't stop. To do that, we need to select the **Loop** option:

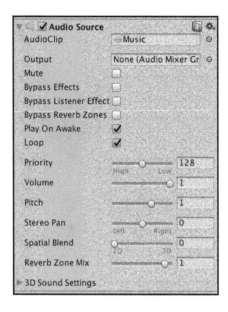

This is very important because if we forget to select this option, the music won't play continuously and it will only play once. Now if we hit the **Play** button, the music will start playing and it won't stop until we restart or close the game.

Adding sound effects

The sounds that we'll be using with more frequency are definitely the sound effects. Everything has a sound: steps, jumps, coins, power–ups, hits, everything, and for that reason, we'll be spending a good amount of time adding sound effects to make our games more pleasing to hear and play.

The most common way to use audio effects is through the animation timeline or through a script. With these two options we should be able to achieve any audio effect that we want, so let's dive into it.

Through animation

Select the `Sprite` of the `Player GameObject` that is inside the **Hierarchy** panel. Go to **Add Component** | **Audio** | **Audio Source**. Click the little circle with a dot inside and now select the audio file that you want to use for the jump effect. Now, we need to make sure to uncheck the **Audio Source** component that we have just added:

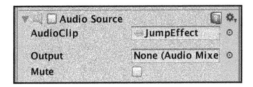

Why? Because we want the audio to be played only when the jump animation starts and if we leave this option selected, it will play right from the start when the character appears on the game, whether he is jumping or not.

Then open the **Animation** window and click where it says **Run**:

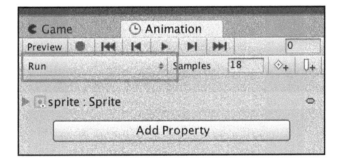

Now, select the **Jump** option:

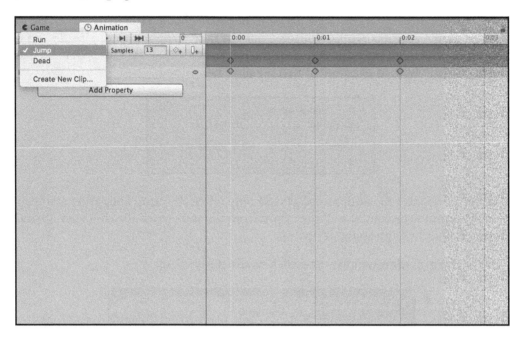

This will open the **Jump** animation that we have created for the character. To edit the animation, remember to click the **Record** button. Now on the first frame, we are going to activate the **Jump** sound effect. To do this, simply check the **Audio Source** box:

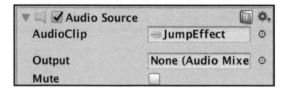

So when the **Jump** animation starts, the **Audio Source** that was disabled gets enabled. For that reason, it starts playing the sound effect and when the animation stops, the **Audio Source** goes back to disabled.

Through script

But what if we want to have multiple effects on a single character? Well, in that case, the most efficient way to do it is by a script. Let's take a look at how to do it.

Open the `PlayerController` script and on the variables section add the following to line **15**:

```
 4  public class PlayerController : MonoBehaviour {
 5
 6      public static PlayerController instance;
 7
 8      public float jumpForce = 6f;
 9      public float runningSpeed = 1.5f;
10      public Animator animator;
11
12      private Vector3 startingPosition;
13      private Rigidbody2D rigidBody;
14
15      public AudioClip killSound;
16
```

This `AudioClip` variable allows us to access an audio file through a script, and we made it public so we can choose it on the Unity editor. Now that we have the variable in place, we need to choose the moment when the sound effect will be played. Judging by the `killSound` variable name, we can see that this will be used the moment that the player character dies. So let's jump to `public void Kill()` and add the updated code here:

```
75      public void Kill() {
76          GameManager.instance.GameOver();
77          animator.SetBool("isAlive", false);
78
79          AudioSource audio = GetComponent<AudioSource>();
80          audio.PlayOneShot(killSound);
81
82          //check if highscore save if it is
83          if (PlayerPrefs.GetFloat("highscore", 0) < this.GetDistance()) {
84              //save new highscore
85              PlayerPrefs.SetFloat("highscore", this.GetDistance());
86          }
87      }
```

As we can see on line **79**, we created an `AudioSource` variable, and then to assign the player character `AudioSource` we used `GetComponent<AudioSource>()`. Then on line **80**, we tell the character to play the `killSound` variable through the `AudioSource` variable that we have selected before.

That's it, the script part is done, but before hitting the Play button, don't forget to assign the desired audio file to the `killSound` variable:

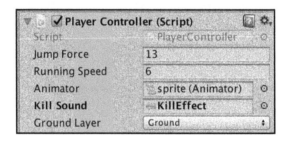

Now if we have a character that has a lot of sound effects to play, we know how to do it, by creating as many `AudioClip` variables as we need and playing them at the moments that we choose.

How to create a 3D game

Creating 2D games is the best option for beginners and that is why we primarily focused on 2D games throughout the book, although almost everything that we have created for the 2D characters and platforms can be applied to 3D as well. But what makes 2D games more friendly to people just learning how to create games? Well, it is easier to find 2D images that we can use as game assets, and because with a simple knowledge of Photoshop, we are able to create our own assets or at least change the ones that we have found on the internet. On the other hand, to create 3D games, we need 3D models and we can also find some of them on the internet, but they need to be rigged if we want them to animate, and the animations need to be created on the 3D programs. Also, it is necessary to create the textures for the models, plus UV mapping the textures. All this takes time and when we start, the best way to learn is by creating many simple games to test different scripts, different components, different ways of creating things.

But when that moment arrives, or if you already have experience with 3D modeling and animation, we'll give you a few fundamentals on how to create a 3D game.

3D models

The models can be downloaded from the internet or created by yourself, and in both cases, it will be necessary to have 3D software to create, edit, and export the files to be used inside Unity. The characters need to have a bone structure attached to them (rig) and the animations should already be created. Once this process is complete, we need to export the 3D files to an .fbx format:

Then on Unity, we go to import and we select the .fbx file that we have just exported. That's it, our 3D model is imported into Unity, and if we want, we can already place it inside the **Hierarchy** panel.

3D animations

After importing the main model into Unity, we can start importing the animation files. Remember that the bone structure, and all the names that we have on the main 3D model, should be exactly the same ones as the animation files, otherwise it won't work at all or it will animate with errors.

On the animation file that we have just imported, if we click it, we can
see the **Animation** tab on the **Inspector** panel. Here it contains all the necessary information
regarding the animation file, where we give a name to the animation and we choose the
duration:

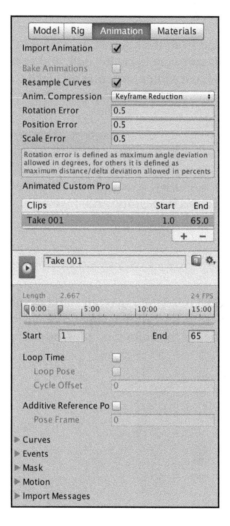

Animator

Once we have all that in place, all we need is to create a new **Animator Controller**, to do this, right-click the **Assets** panel and **Create** | **Animator Controller**:

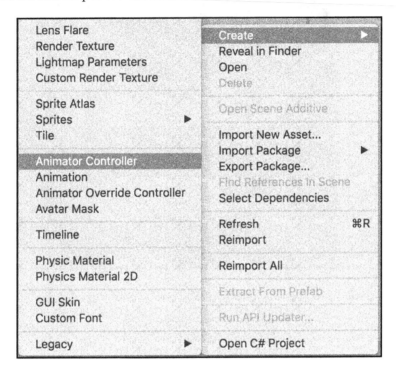

Give it a name and assign it to the character. Open the **Animator** window:

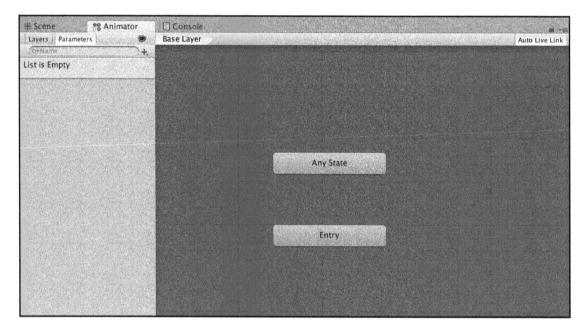

Then, on the animation file, there is an arrow and we click there:

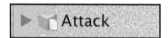

This will open the contents that are present in the file, the one that we want is the animation:

Now, drag and drop the animation inside the **Animator** window:

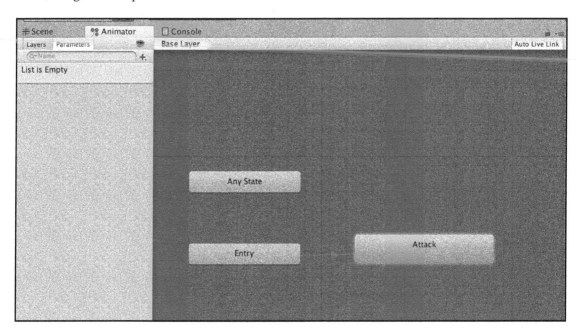

This is all we need to do to import animations into a character. Once we have all the necessary animations inside the **Animator Controller**, we can make them play through a script and use the **Parameters** that can be seen in the **Animator** window.

Because this has a lot of parameters that we can use in order to play the animations and the focus of this chapter is just giving you an introduction to this topic, we highly recommend you check out the official Unity Documentation for this part, as it is vast and very interesting if you want to dive deep into 3D animations: `https://docs.unity3d.com/ScriptReference/Animator.html`.

How to export and make it playable

Exporting the game isn't only used at the end of the development, as it is crucial to export it multiple times to test the game on the devices where the game will be played.

To export the game we need to go to **File** | **Build Settings**. A new window will pop up and this is where we can select the platform that we want:

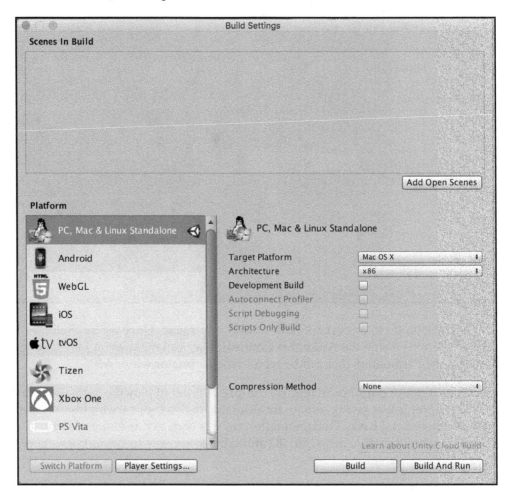

Before clicking the **Build** button, we need to add the scenes that will appear in the game. To do this, we can simply drag and drop them into the empty area on top, or click the **Add Open Scenes** button to add the current scene that we are working on. Once we have done that, we can select the options available on the left. For **Windows** and **Mac OS X** platforms, we can export it right away, as there is no need for any additional content, but for **Android** or **iOS** we need to take a few things into consideration first.

For Android, we need to download `SDK` and `JDK` otherwise we can't export. To do this, we need to go to **Unity | Preferences**, then select the **External Tools** option:

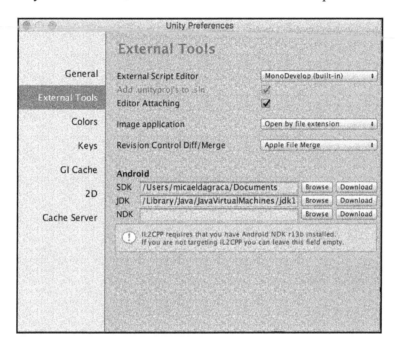

To download the necessary tools, all we've got to do is to click the button that says **Download**, both for `SDK` and for `JDK`. Then you can go back to the **Build Settings** window, select the Android platform, click the **Switch Platform** button and then **Build**.

For **iOS**, you need to be working on a **Mac OS X** computer otherwise you can't export the game to any **iOS** platform. You've also got to have **Xcode** installed on your computer. You can check the official guide on how to export the game to **iOS** using **Xcode**, as this is an **Apple** procedure: `https://unity3d.com/learn/tutorials/topics/mobile-touch/building-your-unity-game-ios-device-testing`.

Code

This section will cover the code that is present in this chapter:

PlayerController.cs

Here's the code:

```
using UnityEngine;
using System.Collections;

public class PlayerController : MonoBehaviour {

    public static PlayerController instance;

    public float jumpForce = 6f;
    public float runningSpeed = 1.5f;
    public Animator animator;

    private Vector3 startingPosition;
    private Rigidbody2D rigidBody;

    public AudioClip killSound;

    void Awake() {
        instance = this;
        rigidBody = GetComponent<Rigidbody2D>();
        startingPosition = this.transform.position;
    }

    public void StartGame() {
        animator.SetBool("isAlive", true);
        this.transform.position = startingPosition;
    }

    void Update () {

        if (GameManager.instance.currentGameState == GameState.inGame)
        {
            if (Input.GetMouseButtonDown(0)) {
                Jump();
            }
            animator.SetBool("isGrounded", isGrounded());
        }
    }

    void FixedUpdate() {

        if (GameManager.instance.currentGameState == GameState.inGame)
        {
            if (rigidBody.velocity.x < runningSpeed) {
```

```
                    rigidBody.velocity = new Vector2(runningSpeed,
rigidBody.velocity.y);
            }
        }
    }

    void Jump() {
        if (isGrounded()) {
            rigidBody.AddForce(Vector2.up * jumpForce,
ForceMode2D.Impulse);
        }
    }

    public LayerMask groundLayer;

    bool isGrounded() {

        if (Physics2D.Raycast(this.transform.position, Vector2.down, 0.2f,
groundLayer.value)) {
            return true;
        }
        else {
            return false;
        }
    }

    void OnCollisionEnter(Collision other) {

        if (other.gameObject.tag == "Enemy") {
            Kill ();
        }
    }


    public void Kill() {
        GameManager.instance.GameOver();
        animator.SetBool("isAlive", false);

        AudioSource audio = GetComponent<AudioSource>();
        audio.PlayOneShot(killSound);

        //check if highscore save if it is
        if (PlayerPrefs.GetFloat("highscore", 0) < this.GetDistance()) {
            //save new highscore
            PlayerPrefs.SetFloat("highscore", this.GetDistance());
        }
    }
```

```
    public float GetDistance() {
        float traveledDistance = Vector2.Distance(new
Vector2(startingPosition.x, 0),
                                                    new
Vector2(this.transform.position.x, 0));
        return traveledDistance;
    }


  }
```

Summary

In this chapter, we have learned how to add music and sound effects into our game, the fundamentals of how to create a 3D game, and finally how to properly export the game so we can play it on different devices.

Now that we have reached the very end of this book, it is time to start exploring everything we have learned so far, combining different elements, changing the scripts that we have created, exploring all the settings for each component and continuing to test new ideas. Don't get discouraged if the game that you have created doesn't look like the one you had in mind, it's completely normal for that to happen, especially at the beginning when we are just learning. Treat every game that you create as a lesson, because you will be always learning new things and you'll be using those new skills on the next game and for every game that you create, a new thing will be implemented and after you've created a few projects, you will feel that it's possible to create anything.

The last piece of advice that I want to give you is don't be ashamed of the games that you create, and don't compare your games with games that were created by teams, where each person is a professional in their field. Create simple games, publish them online to receive feedback, gather a few friends to help you create a more ambitious game, and if you keep doing that, eventually you will gain a few fans or even a legion of them, so don't get discouraged with your first few games, and keep creating new ones.

Index

3

3D animations 262
3D game
  animator 263, 264
  creating 260
3D models 261

A

access modifier 37
animator
  about 151
  executing 153
  PlayerController.cs 154
array
  about 79
  data, retrieving 84
  data, searching 103
  declaring 80
  size, checking 85
  versus List T 83
ArrayList 85
Awake() method 44

B

basic button
  about 199
  button action 200, 201
  button component 199
  image 199
  interaction 200
built-in variable types 61
button 198

C

C# documentation
  about 13
  Unity community 14
C# files
  syncing, between MonoDevelop and Unity 15,
    16
C# script file
  creating 15
  working 14
C# statements
  writing 54
Canvas
  hiding 202
  showing 202
CircleCollider2D 142
class
  about 41
  inheritance 43
code
  conditions, checking in if statement 49
  decisions based, creating on user input 51
  decisions, making 47
  else if, used for making complex decisions 49
  NOT logical operator, used for changing
    condition 48
coin prefab 213, 214
  about 212
  collectable class 216, 217
collectable class 216, 217, 218
collectables 211
component properties
  in Unity's Inspector 55
  Unity changes script 55
  variable names 55
  variables 55

copy of level piece
  creating 184
core components 123
custom constructors 116, 118

D

data
  persisting 219, 220, 221
  retrieving, from array 84
  retrieving, from List T 84
  searching, in array 103
designed level
  creating 175, 176, 178
  LevelGenerator class, planning 180, 181
  script LevelGenerator, writing 182
  versus generated levels 173
dictionaries
  about 87
  Hashtable 89
  values, accessing 88
dot syntax
  about 46
  used, for communicating components 46

E

enemy character 233

F

for loop
  about 94
  condition 94
  example 95, 98
  initializer 94
  iterator 94
  versus while loop 100
foreach loop 92

G

game development
  concept 123, 124
  required skills 122
game mechanics 123
game
  exporting 265, 267

GameObjects
  behavior 10, 11
  Unity's documentation, used 11, 12
Gameplay loops 157, 158, 160
Gameplay
  about 162
  restarting 167
GameView 206, 207
generated level
  creating 179
  versus designed level 173
Graphic User Interface (GUI) 162

H

Hashtable 89
health bar 221, 223
health point 221, 223

I

image 199
inheritance 43
input keys
  setting up 163
Inspector panel
  property's value, changing 56
  public variables, displaying 57
instantiating 185
items
  storing, in list 81

L

level
  extending 188
LevelGenerator
  class, planning 180, 181
  testing 187
List T
  data, retrieving 84
  versus array 83
list
  common operations 83
  items, storing 81
loop
  breaking 104

loops
  about 91
  in statements 100

M

magic bar 223, 224
magic point 223, 224
mechanics
  animated 2D character 127
  collectables 128
  level design 126
  mouse controls 128
  obstacles 128
  physics 128
  scoring 129
  testing 126
  touch controls 128
  user interface 130
method name
  parentheses 70
  with uppercase 69
method parameters
  about 74
  specifying 73
method
  defining 70
  defining, with minimum requirements 70
  multiword names, used 69
  names 40
  naming 69
  used, with object 114, 115
  using 38
  using, in script 68
modulo 102
MonoDevelop code editor
  about 15
  LearningScript, opening 17, 18
  namespace 18
  Project tab 23, 24
  script files, creating in Unity 19, 20
  script, adding to GameObject 20, 21, 22
  simple folder structure 22
  synchronization, fixing 20
movement character
  about 234

animation 234, 236, 237, 238
  enemy character, creating 244
  trigger movement 238, 240, 242, 243
multiword variable names
  using 59
music
  adding 251, 252, 254, 256
  finding 251

N

NOT logical operator 48

O

object
  example 110
  facts 108
  instantiating 111, 112
  method, used 114, 115
  working 105, 107
Objectspan class= 39
overloading 118, 119

P

parentheses 72
player prefab
  CircleCollider2D 142
  preparing 139, 141
  Rigidbody2D 142
player starting position
  setting up 167
PlayerController 143
Private variables 57
property's value
  changing, in Inspector panel 56
public variables
  displaying, in Inspector panel 57

R

reference exceptions 203, 204, 205
resolution 132
Rigidbody2D 142

S

script files
  creating, in Unity 19, 20
script LevelGenerator
  writing 182
scriptphobia
  dealing 8, 9
Singleton class 160
sound effects
  adding 251, 256
  finding 251
  through animation 257, 258
  through script 259, 260
Start() method 44

T

target platform 132
target screen resolution 133
triggers
  using 164, 165

U

Unity community 14
Unity project
  about 137
  backup 136
  setting up, for game 136
Unity UI 194
Unity's documentation
  using 11, 12
Unity's Inspector
  component properties 55
Unity
  downloading 9, 10
  free license, obtaining 10
Update() method 44
user input
  about 144

jump 145, 146, 149, 150

V

value
  assigning, while declaring variable 61
  example 76, 78
  returning 75
  returning, from method 74
variable name
  about 32
  with lowercase 59
variable scope 64
variable
  about 28
  assignment 36
  built-in variable types 61
  changing 37
  creating 34
  declaration 35
  declaring 60, 63
  naming 28, 58
  play button 36
  public variables, using 37
  type 60
  working 34
Vector3
  about 185
  reference link 186
view UI
  constructing 194
view
  about 194
  recognizing events 196
  target screen resolution 195

W

while loop
  about 99
  versus for loop 100